The
Gift of
Asking

Kemi Nekvapil is one of Australia's leading credentialed coaches for female executives and entrepreneurs, an author and a highly sought-after international speaker. She has studied leadership and purpose at the Gross National Happiness Centre in Bhutan as well as with Dr Brené Brown to become a Certified Dare to Lead™ Facilitator, working with teams and organisations to create daring leaders and courageous cultures. Kemi is a facilitator for the Hunger Project Australia and a regular interviewer of industry icons including Elizabeth Gilbert, Martha Beck and Marie Forleo, and she hosts the popular podcast *The Shift Series*. With a level of compassion and wisdom only gained through extraordinary life experience, Kemi is a powerful advocate for connected, value-based living.

keminekvapil.com

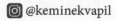 @keminekvapil

KEMI NEKVAPIL

The Gift of Asking

A woman's guide to owning her wants and needs without guilt

PENGUIN LIFE

UK | USA | Canada| Ireland | Australia
India | New Zealand | South Africa | China

Penguin Life is part of the Penguin Random House group of companies
whose addresses can be found at global.penguinrandomhouse.com.

First published by Kemi Nekvapil, 2017
This edition published by Penguin Life, 2022

Copyright © Kemi Nekvapil, 2017, 2022

The moral right of the author has been asserted.

Cover image 'Watercolour Wash' by Bipsun, courtesy Shutterstock
Author photograph by Prue Aja Steedman
Cover design by James Rendall © Penguin Random House Australia Pty Ltd
Text design by Michael Hanrahan Publishing © Penguin Random House Australia Pty Ltd
Typeset in Minion Pro by Midland Typesetters, Australia
Printed and bound in Australia by Griffin Press, an accredited
ISO AS/NZS 14001 Environmental Management Systems printer

A catalogue record for this
book is available from the
National Library of Australia

ISBN 978 1 76104 525 7

penguin.com.au

MIX
Paper | Supporting
responsible forestry
FSC® C018684

We at Penguin Random House Australia acknowledge that Aboriginal and Torres Strait
Islander peoples are the Traditional Custodians and the first storytellers of the lands
on which we live and work. We honour Aboriginal and Torres Strait Islander peoples'
continuous connection to Country, waters, skies and communities. We celebrate
Aboriginal and Torres Strait Islander stories, traditions and living cultures;
and we pay our respects to Elders past and present.

For my children, Benjamin and Ibi.
Thank you for always asking me.
I have grown because of you.
I pray you will always feel worthy enough
to ask for anything.

*'If you don't go after what you want,
you'll never have it.
If you don't ask,
the answer is always no.
If you don't step forward,
you're always in the same place.'*

— **Nora Roberts**

Contents

Preface

Wherever you are in this journey called life, there is a very big chance that within the first few chapters of this book you will become curious about what you are not asking for in your own life and why you are not asking for it.

You will become aware of the impact of not asking on yourself and on those around you, and awareness is the best place to start.

The opening chapters are meant to do this – shine a light on all you have experienced about asking, and all you have been led to believe about asking.

We are all at different stages in our lives; some women find it incredibly easy to ask for anything they want and need, and others, not so much. We can be bold enough to ask for more water at a café, yet be unable to ask for more support around the home. You may find asking for a pay rise easy, but asking for commitment difficult.

You will read about the many reasons why we do not ask, and you will read the personal 'asking stories' of women I interviewed for this book. These women have boldly shared their journeys in the hope that it will elevate you in your journey.

Some of these women are clients I have coached and some are personal friends. In the spirit of sharing honestly and freely, some have chosen to use pseudonyms to protect their privacy.

You will also learn about my asking journey and how it has impacted my life.

By reading different women's stories you will see that wherever you are in life, asking can be a powerful tool for personal growth and for increasing self-worth.

However, every ask and want is not always met with a yes, so you will also find chapters to support you in navigating 'no' responses and to powerfully choose your next step.

I also decided to write a chapter devoted to women saying no. It is impossible to create what we want for ourselves if we are a 'yes' to everyone else.

And of course this book is also about action, because it is action that changes things, not insights. There are five asking processes throughout the book that are designed to get you flexing your asking muscles and introduce you to a new way of living.

It is not until we can face what we have been tolerating, denying and resenting that we can begin to create something else. By the end of this book your relationship to asking will be completely transformed.

My ultimate wish is that this book will play a part in allowing you to own your self-worth and ultimately your life. May you become braver and bolder with every ask.

I have created free resources for you to download. These resources will support you to navigate and explore your asking journey.

Go to kemibooks.com to get yours.

Introduction

Three in one hundred and fifty

I was recently presenting to 150 women at a wellbeing festival, speaking on the subject of women asking for what we need and want. As I spoke, a bold and very personal question that I had not planned to ask came into my head.

'How many of you here in a consensual relationship have only ever had sex when you have genuinely wanted to?'

Of the 150 women in the room, only three of us put up our hands. For whatever reason – and whether it was once, twice or regularly – the other 147 women did not feel they could ask for what they really wanted.

Even though it was their body, they were unable to say, 'I need something else right now.' They didn't feel they could ask, 'Do you think we could just cuddle tonight?' Or 'Would you mind going out to get me some chocolate instead?'

I'd previously been surprised by the revelation of a single woman on the dating scene who basically had sex with men so that she could be cuddled. 'But of course I would never just come out and *ask* for a cuddle,' she said, horrified. '*That* would be weird!'

If I ask, I am…

Even though the specific questions I ask at various speaking events may differ, the response of the majority of my female audiences is always the same.

3

I'll say, 'Who likes to help and support people? Who likes contributing to others?' And every woman puts up her hand.

I then ask, 'Who likes being helped? Who likes being contributed to?' No one raises their hand. No one.

The first time this happened I was so shocked, I posed both questions again. And when I suggested everyone look around to see the obvious imbalance, they too were amazed.

So I asked the group why this imbalance was happening – why we as women struggle to ask for help. This is what they came up with:

> *If I ask, I am weak.*
> *If I ask, I am a burden.*
> *If I ask, I won't get it.*
> *If I ask, I will look stupid.*
> *If I ask, I might get it...*

So I wrote this book

Asking for what we need is not about being selfish or greedy or base. Asking for what we need allows us to live as though we are worthy – because we are.

Whatever we want to achieve in our lives, there will be a certain point we get to where we have to ask for support – if we do not, we cannot move forward. And in asking for support from another person, we expand who they are – we are able to validate their gifts and their unique contribution.

This book is a sharing of my observations as a life coach, and includes personal anecdotes, other women's stories and my suggestions – all intended to show how you can allow yourself to ask for what you need and want.

If you are a woman who rarely asks for what you need or desire, these pages will give you permission to do so.

However, *The Gift of Asking* is not just about elevating your own sense of self – it is also a gift to those who we ask. For, as I mention in my first book, *Raw Beauty*, 'If we refuse contribution from others, we close down their worlds and ours.'

No (wo)man is an island. If we want to contribute to others, achieve our dreams and be fulfilled, we have to allow others to contribute to us.

Asking not only validates your worth, it also validates the worth of the other.

So the gift this book offers is to inspire these thoughts:

'I am worthy enough to ask for help.'
'I am worthy enough to be asked.'

Need or want?

While I was thinking about how to write this book, I struggled for a long time over the difference between 'needing' and 'wanting'. I wrestled with my own long-held belief that to 'need' is right, proper and pure, whereas to 'want' is greedy, unnecessary and selfish. Both words, I realised, are pretty loaded.

How do the words 'want' and 'need' make you feel? If the first stirs up thoughts of bad people being greedy, and the latter of good people being virtuous, you are not alone. It is extremely common for women to make this association.

We all need things that allow us to be fully present in our lives, and these needs differ for each woman. When these needs are met we are able to live the full expression of ourselves.

Working out what constitutes a need (versus a want) and how to rank its importance can be quite complex, too. Our need for love is more important than our need for a kitchen table, for example, but most people want and need both. And some people may believe that our need for good health is more important than our need for fun, but most people want and need both.

To complicate things further, in acknowledging and satisfying our needs we do not want to be seen as weak and burdensome – we do not want to be known as 'needy'.

It felt like walking through a mine field so, for the purposes of this book, I have chosen to use the word 'need' most of the time. To need in the moment, to need in the long term, and to need without guilt or apology.

We all have needs. The basic universal ones – food, shelter and safety – go hand in hand with our emotional and spiritual need to feel loved, to feel heard, to be validated, to feel seen, and to feel valued and supported.

None of these needs makes us weak; in fact, they all make us kinder people – kinder to others and to ourselves.

I will also use the word 'want' as necessary since we all have perfectly reasonable wants and need not be ashamed of them.

Whether it is a need or a want, or something in between, having it fulfilled is not a birthright. And this book is about making it happen – through acting on it and asking.

Creating with courage

None of us deserves a life that is automatically fulfilling – we need to create our own fulfilled existence as individuals. It takes work, practice and commitment, as well as vulnerability, courage and bravery. It includes failure and upset, and trying again. It is not always comfortable or easy, but it is always worth it.

Every time we complain about what someone else is or is not doing, it is a great opportunity to look at what we are or are not doing. It is a good time to ask ourselves these questions:

'Am I asking or am I settling for what is easy?'
'Am I fulfilled or am I frustrated?'
'Am I doing or am I hoping?'

We can spend so much energy and time complaining, when we could be creating a much better outcome through asking and doing.

Of course, it takes courage to take action; it always has and always will. It also takes bravery to state what you need. And it requires immense vulnerability to ask for more than what has been dealt out to you.

Most importantly, it takes feeling worthy.

Feeling your worth

Worthiness is at the core of so many decisions we make about ourselves and others. It is the foundation of how we treat ourselves and how we treat others. It dictates and defines what we feel we deserve in all areas of life – who we have as friends, who we choose as a life partner, who we do business with, where we go, what careers we have and how we experience the world.

But worthiness is a tricky concept. Who can say whether I am worthy? Who decides if you are worthy?

The fact is other people cannot pronounce you or me worthy. Not our friends, partners, parents, children or work colleagues.

So next time you catch yourself putting your worthiness into the hands of others, stop. Your self-worth is too big a burden for another person to carry – it is your responsibility to nurture and manage.

Active asking

Action changes everything. For example, the action of asking for what we need catapults us into a place of worthiness and value. So instead of waiting to be worthy enough to ask for what you need, ask away and in the process you will become worthy. When you find yourself in certain situations, ask yourself:

> *'Do I value myself enough to ask?'*
> *'Am I worthy enough to state my preference in this situation?'*

We will not always get what we ask for – and sometimes that is for the best – but we will always build our worthiness just by taking the action of asking in the first place.

The cost of not asking

There is no end to the list of reasons we give for not asking for what we need and want. Here are some more reasons that women have shared with me. How many ring true for you?

> *I do not want to look greedy.*
> *I am too scared.*
> *I am afraid of getting a no.*

I am afraid of getting a yes.
I am afraid of looking stupid.
I am scared of being rejected.
I do not want to appear arrogant.
I do not want to be a burden.

We may think it is simply easier not to ask, since we do not want to be rejected, embarrassed or to feel uncomfortable. However, the impact on women of *not* asking for what we need and want seems much more profound. These are just some of the consequences of not asking:

- Building resentment
- Constant disappointment
- Anger
- The need to blame
- Withdrawing from others
- Shutting down
- Nagging
- Testing
- Punishing
- Suffering and causing others to suffer
- Hoping instead of doing
- Tolerating
- Feelings of failure
- Feelings of jealousy
- Judging of others
- Gossiping
- Feeling like a victim

What are you not asking for, and what is the impact of this inability to ask on your day-to-day wellbeing and experience of life?

How I improved my ask-ability

We have all had certain life experiences where we asked for something and we got a no, a rejection. It could have sounded like this: 'Who do you think you are to ask that?' 'Be grateful for what you have.' 'If you ask for help, people will think you are weak.' 'Never ask for anything.' 'If you ask for anything, you are being selfish.'

I had many versions of this throughout my childhood, some of which I will share with you later. Let me just say, my biggest barrier to asking for what I wanted was my own internal voice. I used to believe that if you wanted a job done properly, it was best to do it yourself. This left me feeling exhausted and resentful, which is not a fulfilling place to be.

Luckily for me, I married an 'asker' – although sometimes what he asks for embarrasses me, and what I ask for embarrasses him, because we both need and desire different things.

During 12 months of travelling around Australia in a caravan with our two children, the two of us explored asking for what we wanted and many doors opened to us that might otherwise have remained closed – not just externally but within our marriage as well. We are very clear on what each other needs at various times because we ask each other often. We do not spend time guessing; we ask.

I have taught my children to ask for what they want, too; that if they do not ask it is always a no, but if they do ask they may get a yes or another opportunity may be presented to them.

My youngest is the ultimate asking master; my eldest has learned to ask more, after he realised that if he does not ask he misses out.

Are you an asker?

Like so much in life, our ability – or inability – to ask for what we need and want depends on our external and internal programming. Like so many women, your life experience and internal responses may have rendered you mute as far as expressing your needs goes. Maybe you do ask, but only to a certain point.

I once had a client who gave herself permission to have a massage (a big step for her), but when she got to her appointment the room was too cold, she did not like the music being played, the massage was not deep enough and she could not relax. Even though the therapist had told her to ask if she wanted anything changed, she did not ask.

This woman had been looking forward to some self-care – which she had paid for – but she was afraid to ask for what she needed. So in the end she did not get what she wanted, and was left feeling frustrated and disappointed.

It was only once we were discussing this during a session that she realised she rarely asked for what she wanted and constantly found herself disappointed.

The reason the therapist asked the client to ask for what she needed was so that she – the therapist – could do her best work. But because the client did not state her needs, neither she nor the therapist got what they wanted.

The art of asking

When we ask, we can be shifted into another dimension – one where the world is full of people who say yes, and where the ones who say no have only said no. They have not said no to us as a person; they have said no to the ask.

Once you start feeling the power of asking openly, it will trigger all sorts of exciting possibilities. You will start thinking, maybe I need to ask someone else. Maybe I need to ask for less, ask differently, or maybe I need to put some more work in and ask again at another time.

By not asking to start with, many women reject their needs and wants long before anyone else has the chance to do so. These women might think:

'There is no point in me asking, I know what they are going to say.'
'I am not good enough to ask for that.'
'They will say no, so why bother?'
'I already asked and they said no.'

Something I learnt a long time ago is that I have no idea what someone else's answer is going to be unless I ask them. Everything else we decide is an assumption, either based on our take on the current situation, or based on something that happened in the past.

For many of us it feels safer to assume that we know what the answer will be than to actually ask the question in the first place. But we need to keep in mind that we have all had no for an answer before and that we have all survived worse, and unless we ask the question, we will never know the answer.

When we ask for what we need, we cultivate a lighter energy for ourselves and those around us. We experience a greater sense of flow and ease by asking for support from others, and we experience an increased level of worthiness and personal power.

So my message to you in this book is simple and powerful.

'Ask.'

Chapter 1
The issue of asking

Over the past few years while working with women as a life coach, I have noticed a recurring issue. It keeps showing up again and again, and it is an issue too obvious to ignore.

It does not matter who I am working with, what the issue is that my client and I are navigating together or what stage of life they are in, we seem to hit on the same issue repeatedly.

It is when we get to the point where the client needs to ask for something – a thing they need or want to be able to move themselves forward – that we encounter a barrier.

It can be anything – the need to ask for help, time, money, feedback, hugs. And I say something like, 'Have you considered *asking* for what you want?'

At this moment, one of two things tends to happen. Either the client sees they had no idea that asking was a possibility in their situation, or they hit up against an internal barrier that prevents them from asking for what they want.

It is not the case for every single client, but it has happened enough for me to see that we women generally have a fear of asking.

What is it about asking?

Why do we struggle so much when it comes to asking for what we need and want?

Life can be brimming with joy, fulfilment, flow, magic and adventure. It can also be filled with loss, struggle, heartbreak and pain.

All of us will move through every one of these spaces and more during our life, and one of the most effective ways to navigate that journey – to steer yourself towards the good bits and find your way out of the bad ones – is to ask for what you need and want.

If you want more passion from your partner, you have to ask for it.

If you want a new role at work, you need to ask for the promotion.

If you have suffered the loss of someone you love through death or a break up and you need space to grieve, you need to ask for that space. (How will the people thinking you want company all the time know otherwise?)

If you have just lost your job and everyone keeps asking you how the job-hunting is going, you can ask them to stop asking if it makes you feel bad.

If you are asked to make a major life decision and you need more time to weigh up the options, you can ask for more time.

If we do not ask, we begin to create a whole world of suffering for ourselves.

The suffering can sound like: 'They will not leave me alone...', 'They always pass me over for promotion...', 'They are an ineffective team...', 'They are pressuring me to make a decision.'

If we constantly expect others to guess what it is we need or want (see Chapter 3, The mind readers), instead of being willing and able to consistently ask for what we need or want, a lifetime of suffering is guaranteed.

This way of living – where we are veering haphazardly, being run by circumstances and having no real say about our direction or destination – does not allow us to be in the driving seat of our own lives. And sitting in the back seat of an out-of-control life rarely provides opportunities for thriving or growth.

On a personal level, meanwhile, relationships rarely thrive and grow when the person we love has no idea about what we need or want.

So it's just a matter of asking?

Yes. But for many of us, 'just asking' is not simple or obvious.

I will always remember the lady I met at a presentation I was giving who put her hand up to ask a question, then put it down, and then put it up again and said:

'My husband and I have been together for 25 years – surely he should know what I want by now!'

I was moved by her level of frustration, and I felt for her husband.

'No,' I said. 'He will have no idea of what you want unless you tell him – and you will never get what you need unless you ask for it.'

I also mentioned the chance that who she is now, and who he is now, is probably different to who they were 25 years ago.

She agreed and asked, 'So I just have to ask him?'

'Yes,' I replied. 'And while you are telling him what you need, you may want to ask him what he needs.'

'I had never thought of that,' she admitted. 'I am constantly disappointed in him for not giving me what I want, but I had never thought that maybe I am not giving him what he wants.'

'And how does that make you feel?' I asked.

'It makes me a little sad that I never thought to ask him,' she revealed. 'But it also makes me feel excited. This could be a really exciting new chapter for us.'

And I felt quite excited for them both, too. Because as I say over and over again, asking is not just about the 'asker', it is also about the person being asked.

Honestly, we give so much to another person when we ask them a question from a place of possibility and opportunity. It gives us the chance to understand each other's worlds better, and the opportunity to have open and authentic conversations. It also allows for the chance to take action if action is the next step.

Chapter 2
The women who asked

Need is not greed. Agreed?

Throughout history and in recent times, on the streets in public rallies and in homes using their personal power, women who asked for their rights and the satisfaction of their own and their communities' needs made change happen.

The Suffragettes – a women's movement that started in the 1890s – had to ask for the right to vote because there was no way it was just going to be given to them.

Malala Yousafzai – a young Pakistani girl – had to ask for an education because no one was going to give it to her. She went on to become the youngest ever Nobel Prize laureate and changed the future of millions of girls and young women around the globe through her activism.

The women in India who founded an organisation called Right to Pee had to ask for toilets to be built in their villages because they

19

were sick and tired of the real threat of sexual assault every time they had to go outside to pee.

All of these women had to ask for what they wanted and needed in terrible circumstances, and sometimes with near-fatal repercussions. But without their courage to ask, so many people's lives would not have improved.

The right to vote, go to school and pee in safety is taken for granted by many of us. Yet these basic rights for women were once not seen as rights at all, and the women who started to ask for them out loud were seen as noisy and greedy and selfish. But while it is now easy to see that these 'greater' needs were worth asking for, most women struggle with their right or worthiness to ask for their 'smaller' personal needs.

Becoming a 'greedy' woman

If any of these women had thought that asking was a selfish act – if they had thought they were being greedy – nothing would have changed. Nothing at all.

Many of the chapters in this book describe reasons why we as women find it incredibly hard, if not impossible, to ask for what we need. Yet I believe that if we each worked on asking for something that is important for ourselves as individuals, to make our personal situation better in some way, in the end our asking would change other people's lives positively too.

Where and how your power of asking breaks through and takes hold will depend on your circumstances. A seemingly 'greedy' request for a late checkout from a hotel may in turn empower you to eventually ask for other things that can make a huge difference to your family, workplace, community and humankind. Or perhaps asking for that late checkout will allow you the time to have a conversation or be somewhere that is life-changing.

But whether you just want to make your life in your little patch of this planet better, or you want to change the world, you need to be able to ask for what you need to make it happen.

Middle-class guilt does not change anything; action does.

Poverty-shame does not change anything; action does.

A woman asking for a late checkout from a place of self-worth is no less than a woman asking for a toilet in her village from a place of self-worth.

Both women are asking for what they need and want. Both women are in their power. Both women are worthy.

So are you.

Chapter 3
The mind readers

They do not exist.

Chapter 4
The cost of not asking

Before we get further into the act of asking for what we need or want, I want to explore the cost of not doing so.

If you skipped the introduction to this book and you still believe that asking for what you want is selfish, greedy or frivolous, I am here to show you otherwise. The inability to ask for what we need or want has a big impact on how we experience ourselves, what we feel we deserve and how we relate to other people. It affects our lives in a big way.

This is what happens

The list that follows is a detailed version of the one in the Introduction, and as you read it you might like to make a mental note of which of these feelings or emotional states occur for you when you are unable to ask for what you want, what you desire, what you need.

Feeling unfulfilled

When we believe we have to do everything on our own, there is no way that we can fulfil our deepest dreams. It is important to have others supporting us along the way, and not asking for this support can leave us feeling unfulfilled in many areas of our lives.

We all have unique talents and abilities that will get us to a certain point in our lives. For example, we may begin our parenting journey very well and sail through the first couple of years, and then when the 'defiant toddler' stage hits we feel out of our depth; instead of sailing through, now we feel as if we are drowning. At this point we need to ask for the support of others with different or better abilities to help us to move forward. Unless we do, we can be unfulfilled in our parenting role – and as parenting is for life, it is a long time to be feeling unfulfilled.

The same goes for our work. How many people are unfulfilled in their work lives?

Feeling disappointed

The feeling of being constantly disappointed by others is emotionally draining and can cause our closest relationships to crumble. Not letting someone important to you know what you need from them sets up a state of chronic disappointment for you and a constant feeling of failure in them – neither of which will support a healthy relationship. And if we are not careful, the disappointment we feel can become a permanent state of being.

Hoping instead of doing

Hoping that something will turn out how you want it to without actually expressing what you need is a recipe for failure. Hope is different to trust, and constantly hoping that something is going to turn out leaves you at the mercy of circumstances. We have more control than we often believe we do; but sometimes taking control is scarier than hoping, so we continue to hope and nothing changes.

Feeling lonely

Not asking for what you need may promote feelings of independence for a while, but can leave you feeling lonely in the long term. No (wo)man is an island unless she decides that she is. As we become accustomed to not asking for support, input or feedback, we have more of life's 'stuff' to carry on our own backs, and in turn people see us carrying so much and believe therefore that we do not need support, so they never offer.

Remember, if we create the sense that we can do it all alone, we will find ourselves alone.

Lacking a sense of worth

Feelings of worthlessness look different for different women at different times. We can feel worthy in some situations but not in others. But if we feel unworthy a majority of the time, we will experience constant negative emotions that will have an impact on our sense of self and wellbeing, which in turn will direct what we will and will not ask for.

Withdrawing and shutting down

If we continue to deprive ourselves of what we need through not asking, the constant feelings of disappointment, loneliness, unworthiness and lack of fulfilment will cause us to withdraw into ourselves and shut down from those around us. Never asking. Never risking. Never truly connecting. Never fully living.

Nagging

We nag when we are not getting what we want – which is difficult for the person at the receiving end if we have not told them what it is we want. The only thing worse than being nagged at is being the person who is doing the nagging, as it robs us of our sense of the person we want to be. Nagging puts a distance between us and those we love, and is usually followed by regret. The simple solution: check whether you have actually asked for what you need.

Testing

This used to be one of my personal favourites. I would set up a particular 'test' for someone. If they do not call by…If they do not do the dishes by…If they have not said xxxx by…then I will xxxx.

If they did not pass the test – a test they knew nothing about, mind you – I would generally punish them in some way, usually by withdrawing and not speaking to them. (One of my foster mothers told me about the time I did not speak to her for three days. It was an incredibly hard time for her and, of course, I have apologised since, but it was incredibly hard for me, too, as I had to pretend I hated her.) Childish, yes – it is a trick we learned in childhood and it is how I survived.

I wish we had all been taught how to ask for what we needed in childhood instead.

Suffering and causing others to suffer

We kid ourselves that we suffer in silence (oh, the martyrdom of it) but generally we will share what is 'being done to us', and how we are being taken for granted, used, ignored or passed over with anyone who will listen. So there are potentially three people suffering – you, the person who is listening to you, and possibly the person who is 'doing' this to you because they sense a change in the relationship (even though they have no idea what has happened).

Rather than suffering in so-called silence, you can make your expectations clear and express any disappointment directly to the person who can make the difference in that situation.

Being resentful

Resentment and its subcategories of jealousy and bitterness usually erupt from what someone else has that you do not – going on frequent holidays, for example, or being in a relationship, or having career success or good health. We see someone else with what we want or need, and instead of thinking 'I am going to ask for that!' (increased holiday hours, for example), which takes vulnerability and risk, we divert that possible action into a negative emotion aimed at the person who has what we want: 'I cannot believe they are going on holiday again. I work so much harder than them.'

Being judgemental

You may know the saying that every time you point a finger at someone else there are three fingers pointing right back at you.

Judging is a great way of not asking for our needs to be met. If we are focused on what someone else is or is not doing, we do not have to take action ourselves.

We may say, 'They are so arrogant, how can they ask for *that*?' When what we actually mean is, 'I wish I had the guts to ask for that!'

We judge as a way to avoid what is going on for us. Life is so fragile and sometimes extremely hard. I believe that everyone is doing the best they can with what they have at that time, in terms of experience, resources and knowledge. It is possible to be where the 'other' is, to have what the 'other' has, but it takes effort and action and commitment. Do not waste energy judging others when you could be using that energy to create your own life.

Gossiping

Sadly, gossiping is such a huge part of our culture, there are entire magazines, television shows and websites dedicated to it. Gossiping can be an offshoot of jealousy, envy and bitterness, and being a gossip says more about the gossiper than the person being gossiped about.

When we spend our time gossiping about the mother who has her young child in childcare, while we are struggling to have a shower each day because our baby never sleeps, maybe we are the ones who need to ask for support. It may not be the same kind of support, but we need to ask nonetheless.

Gossiping to others does not get our needs met. All gossiping does is leech us of our basic kindness and empathy.

Feeling disempowered

When we feel disempowered we experience life not as something we are creating but as something that is happening to us; that we have to roll with the punches whatever they are and suck it up.

More dangerous than that is the disempowered notion that someone or something is coming to save us. Empowered thinking comes with the knowledge that only we can make the changes we want in our lives.

Blaming

It is so tempting to play the blame game. If it can be someone else's fault that you are not living the life you want, it removes all responsibility from you.

'I don't have this and I don't have that.' Have you asked for this and that? Have you shared your needs? Have you offered someone the opportunity to support you? When we claim full responsibility for our lives it means that we are in charge and we have to take action – which is much scarier than being able to blame someone else.

Being angry

Feelings of being put upon, taken for granted or not recognised for what you do can all lead to feelings of anger. While anger does not have to be a bad or negative emotion, it can be the fuel that stokes an internal fire, and it can change the world. When that anger is held onto, when the energy of it is not used to shift or change something, it festers and kills. It kills our spirit, narrows our perception and alters our soul.

We are allowed to ask to be recognised and we are allowed to ask for acknowledgement. Our anger has no positive impact on our lives unless we decide to employ it to fuel positive change.

What am I not asking for?

Did you identify with any of these costs?

You probably noticed as you read this list that many of the costs feed each other. If we are constantly disappointed, we start to test; if we are constantly testing, we feel unfulfilled; if we are constantly unfulfilled, we withdraw, which makes us lonely, and so on.

Maybe there is only one of the above that you have identified with, or you may feel you have ticked all the boxes.

So, when you are going about your day, have a personal check-in to see what you are feeling and whether you can trace that feeling back to the above 'costs' list.

This will allow you to begin the process of asking the all-important question:

'What am I not asking for that is making me feel this way?'

Tantalika's asking story

I still struggle with asking because you were not supposed to ask.

I grew up in South Africa and for six years I was the last born in my family. I got away with a lot. After my younger brother came, my parents separated and everything changed.

Whatever situation I was in I had to be grateful and good. Asking equalled rudeness or ungratefulness.

Where I am from, as a girl in a household with a married couple I had to ask my mother or aunt to deliver my messages to my father or uncle. I could not approach my dad, but my uncle was almost maternal to me so I just went straight to him and got what I wanted, and it was awesome.

My uncle was lovely and I could ask him anything and it was fine, but whoever his current wife or girlfriend was found it disrespectful – they felt I skipped a necessary channel to him.

So I became timid and was scared all the time. A painful memory for me is when I was in grade two and I think l ate some bad food that gave me diarrhoea. Crippled with anxiety and not able to say anything, I crapped my pants and knew I had to fix it myself. I was so afraid to ask for help, I dug a hole and hid the underwear.

These days I have a son who is autistic and incontinent so I must clean him up all the time, and it reminds me of that situation every day. I am glad it is not him in my shoes those years ago, and I do not want him to fall into a trap of not asking. Although my son cannot speak, he always asks in his way. I always ask him as well.

When I was his age, to me asking was impolite. Sometimes it still feels like that, and I have cruised through letting the people around me do the asking without me saying anything. I will only ask when pushed to the extreme, when it comes across as very blunt or almost comes out as a demand.

You see, asking just was not something you did. It was rude to ask.

There are things I wish I had asked for, though. I wish I had asked my mother for the tools I needed for my technical graphics class. I decided she could not afford them, and went back to school and told my teacher that we were struggling.

I wish I had asked my ex-husband to leave the first few weeks we started dating.

If I did ever ask, often I felt a lot of unpleasantness from being rejected or I was asked why I was even asking in the first place. Asking was not respecting your elders.

Asking meant you had to be prepared to exchange something to the giver's benefit. Asking meant I had failed to acquire the things on my own that I wanted, and that came across as weak, unqualified or unknowledgeable. Asking was too forward. If I fancied a man and asked to spend time with him, it would be too forward or I would be interpreted as being a 'fast' woman.

Choices were made for me when I did not ask, so whatever situation I was in, it was without my choosing. My life was an accumulation of choices and decisions made on my behalf.

Even now I get anxious asking for something that I really want.

I often find myself in tense conversations when I eventually decide to ask for what I want or need. This is because, when I am slow to ask, the giver will have already made the final decision and assumed that my not asking before was my way of saying I was happy with what was going on.

Over my life I have often felt hopeless for not asking for the things I want or need, but now I know asking is asking. I have learnt that it is not a transaction unless the person you ask specifically asks for it to be. I have learned that if you must ask, just do it and get over it, do not procrastinate.

I grew up reading the Bible. 'Ask and it will be given unto you,' the Bible says.

Asking changes things in my life. I am more aware of what it means, and that it is a word that I can use at will. Asking is empowering – it means I can get things done with a clear head and no guilt.

Tantalika, 30

Chapter 5
Good girls do not ask

I spoke about the curse of the 'good girl' and the impact it has on women in my first book, *Raw Beauty*. This curse prevents us from living fully passionate and nourishing lives.

Many of us were raised to be good girls: 'Never make a fuss.' 'Do not upset anyone.' 'Do not draw attention to yourself.' 'Do not rock the boat.' 'Be good.'

One of the perceived rewards for being good in our culture is that we get to be labelled as 'nice'. Not passionate, or determined, or ambitious, or having integrity, but nice.

The curse of the good girl must never be underestimated, because it is all-pervasive and it has allowed for women to be kept in check for a very long time. It still exists, it still cages us, and – consciously or unconsciously – we all have the need to be a 'good girl' in some areas of our lives. As good mothers, good daughters, good partners, good wives, good bosses, good employees.

The reality is there is no such thing as a 'good girl', and trying to live in a role that we believe will make us more lovable is a sure way to lose who we really are in the process.

It is impossible to be just one thing all the time, not to mention emotionally tiring and physically exhausting.

Who can be 'good' all the time and who defines what the parameters of good are anyway? Who can be passionate all the time? Who can be happy all the time?

What an incredible amount of pressure to put on oneself. As women we are multi-layered. We are all a bit of everything depending on the circumstances we find ourselves in, which is natural and healthy and human and allowed.

When good girls sweat

I recently watched a wonderful documentary called *Free to Run*, which told the story of the women who were allowed to run the marathon distance for the first time in the 1984 Olympic Games. Previously women had not been allowed to run this race for fear a uterus or two might fall out on the home stretch. True.

Gabriela Andersen-Schiess, a Swiss runner in this marathon event, had memorably pushed herself so hard and was so dehydrated she basically zig-zagged from side to side, bent over in a very crooked position, for the last lap of the stadium. Not very good-girlish at all!

Kathrine Switzer, who was the first lady to run the Boston Marathon, nailed it when she said, 'One of the most amazing things about the 1984 Olympic marathon is that it allowed women to be exhausted in public.'

There are still so many rules around what women should and should not do.

But the truth and reality is, we can be angry and direct *and* graceful, harsh *and* resourceful, beautiful *and* tired. We can be scared *and* sexual, confused and lost *and* strong.

Anything other than a full range of human expression is a constructed cage that is dehumanising and dangerous for any woman or girl.

And because of all of this, I believe mothers of daughters need to be mindful of using labels like 'good girl' – we want them to know they are so much more than that. They are allowed to be more.

When being good means feeling bad

So how does being a 'good girl' relate to us not asking for what we need? In my experience, and that of many of my clients, there are many barriers to breaking out of 'good girl' mode and asking for what we need and want. Here are just some of those barriers – and the labels they attract if we dare jump over or push through them.

- We are worried about what other people will think about us – 'She is a bad girl.'
- We do not want to be seen as greedy – 'I cannot believe she asked for more!'
- We do not want to appear arrogant – 'She is so full of herself!'
- We do not want to be seen as bossy – 'She is so bossy!'
- We do not want to be seen as too successful – 'Who does she think she is?'
- We do not want to be gossiped about – 'Did you hear what she did!?'
- We do not want to be seen as lazy – 'I cannot believe she thinks she deserves more time off than the rest of us.'

And the list goes on and on – you will probably have your own versions, and more.

So you see how our need to 'be good' has a far-reaching impact on how we act in the world, what we think we are worthy of and what we think we deserve. And all of this directly influences what we feel we are allowed to ask for and who we are allowed to ask.

Most of us have been trained to think the need to be this society-ready and ever-obedient good girl overrides all other needs we might have. It is time to shed the good girl persona, get in touch with the real woman you are, and ask for the things that matter to you.

Chapter 6

A martyr never asks

'If you had a "martyr mother", please put your hand up.'

This is one of the questions I ask in my Raw Beauty Masterclass, and generally at least half of the women in the room will put their hands up in response to it.

The *Oxford Dictionary* gives the following definitions and descriptions of a martyr:

> '*A person who displays or exaggerates their discomfort or distress in order to obtain sympathy...*'

> '*Those who love to play the martyr submerge their own personalities. They devote a lifetime to unnecessary servitude and privation...*'

> '*Some parents put their children first in order to play the martyr.*'

These descriptions are very telling, and they are the lived experience of many children of a particular generation of mothers. A mother's martyr-like behaviour affects her children – and especially her daughters – in largely negative ways their entire lives.

The next question I ask is, 'If your mother's martyrdom served you in a positive way, please keep your hand up.'

All hands go down, with a lot of head-shaking.

The cost of martyrdom

'Why did your mother's martyrdom not work for you?' I ask.

One of the things I love about speaking and facilitating groups is how it can create a space where women can feel safe enough to reflect on their lives – to have the time to look at where they have been, what they have learnt along the way and what they want for the future.

These are thoughts women have shared about their mothers' martyr-like behaviour:

> *'I was made to feel that my mother's whole existence was purely for me. It was a great burden.'*
>
> *'I had to watch my mother belittling herself and her worth. It seemed she felt that was the only way she got attention.'*
>
> *'I felt responsible for my mother's happiness. I was unable to live my life fully until she passed away.'*
>
> *'I watched my mother make herself extremely ill because she was unable to ask for any help or support. Even though I saw the impact it had on her and her marriage, I am my mother's daughter and I struggle with asking for help too.'*

The alternative to martyrdom

We no longer have to be 1950s housewives – unless we want to be. I chose to be 'mother and homemaker' for seven years, but then I wanted something else.

But first I had to give myself permission to want more, and then I had to ask for help so that I could make it happen. I needed to find a level of childcare that I was happy with, so a woman from a nanny agency started coming to our house once a week to look after the children. This allowed me to have the space to ask and think about the questions 'What do I want to birth into the world?' and 'What do I want to contribute?'

Of course, we can do it all ourselves, without help – we are women and since the beginning of time we have had to do many, many things alone. It is proven that we are the best multi-taskers, but it has also been proven that multi-tasking is not effective and can impact our wellbeing, our focus, our relationships and our self-esteem. Multi-tasking has us doing a lot but we do not feel good about anything we are doing. At the end of the day we are exhausted – we have been busy but we have no sense of fulfilment or joy.

The guilt factor

Another aspect of becoming a martyr is that we can unknowingly use guilt to get people to help us.

You may find yourself saying, 'No one ever helps me!' or 'I always have to do everything myself!'

I know for myself that whenever I have felt like this, it has been because I have been living the lie that I have to do everything myself. And this lie leaves me feeling overwhelmed, lonely and struggling.

'Guilting' people into helping us is not a great strategy. You never really get what you want, which is equal partnership and collaboration, and when people offer from a place of guilt, it leaves them feeling resentful and angry. So both the asker and the 'askee' are swimming in overwhelm, loneliness, struggle, guilt, resentment and anger. What a team!

Life beyond martyrdom

Do you find yourself operating from a place of martyrdom? What is the impact on you? What is the impact on those around you?

Alarm bells may have rung as you read this chapter. You will know whether you have adopted some martyrdom tendencies, and you will know who you inherited them from. It could have been any of the female role models in your life, or due to a personality you have constructed to survive something or someone.

Ultimately, though, whatever we have inherited, we are now adults and we are able to choose. We get to put our big girl panties on now.

Every single chapter in this book is an opportunity to look at where you currently see yourself in relation to asking. It is only when we can be honest with where we are now that we can begin to make changes. Awareness is power and sometimes awareness is all we need.

Recognising and then owning the patterns that we have inherited or constructed is the first step towards another way; a way that makes life not only more fulfilling, but a joyous creation.

Amy's asking story

As a child I learnt that if I asked nicely, I had a far better chance of getting what I wanted. Manners were very important in our household and they got us a long way.

My parents were quite firm with my siblings and me. They taught us to speak directly, not to beat around the bush; they did not stand for whining or 'fluffy' round-about ways of asking for what we wanted. I guess this has impacted my communication style markedly, in light of the fact I am now anything but fluffy.

I also learnt that having your best friend next to you when you asked your parents if she could have a sleepover was not a good tactic. In fact, it just made them cross.

After living away from my parents as an adult for decades, I eventually moved back home with them so I could be looked after.

In 2010 I was diagnosed with chronic fatigue syndrome after a slow decline in health over many years. In the end it was so bad that I could not look after myself, and I walked away from a successful business and ultimately went to Tasmania to live with my parents.

Following my diagnosis and before the inevitable move back 'home', I was housebound and terribly lonely. Any sort of stimulation, be it television, music, loud noise or groups of people, wore me down dreadfully.

Some days I could not manage to hold my hands up above my head to wash my hair, but I still could not ask for help – not even just to have someone drop around some food.

In hindsight, I wish I'd had the courage to ask for help when I really needed it. I wish I had not been too proud to seek the company of friends who would have been perfectly happy to sit quietly on the couch with me.

I wish I had not felt the need to prove that I was always so ridiculously capable and strong.

I never asked because I had never asked before. I had always done everything on my own. That was who I was; the fiercely independent, totally capable 'doer' who had always managed alone, and who did not need anyone else for anything.

I also felt that I was not alone in my difficulties. Everyone has challenges, everyone has burdens – did they also need mine? I did not think so at the time.

I actually recall one day immediately following my diagnosis, while I was trying to hold onto any semblance of independence by living alone, having no food in the house. Somehow I had to get myself to the markets. Things were so bad that simply turning the steering wheel in the car was a battle (one of my arms was often in a sling because it hung limply by my side).

I will never forget that day, driving home in tears because I knew what was to come as a result of pushing myself over and over again.

Instead of asking for help I made that trip to the markets – and paid the price by having to spend the following week totally exhausted in bed. This was a common story and the cost was my health.

The biggest ask of my life was of my parents when I finally realised I could not do it on my own anymore.

Even though my parents had frequently insisted that I live with them during recovery, it still felt like an ask – I still felt like a burden. But it was clear that I had no choice; I could not survive on my own.

They supported me financially, they fed me and they did my washing. When I was well enough they let me live in their holiday house to learn to cope on my own again. What they did for me felt HUGE – overwhelmingly so.

But I gained a lot from the experience. Living with my parents enabled me to 'project manage' my recovery, which was the very best thing for an A type like me. All I had to think about was getting well and it was almost indulgent. I set myself 12 months to get my life back and I had all bases covered.

In return, not only did I recover, but I gained so much through the renewed connection with my wider family.

I was learning for the first time as an adult how to ask for help. I cannot tell you how the burden was lifted in those simple requests.

And now I know and fully understand the joy that comes from helping others – the beautiful energy that flows from us when we are in service. Knowing the joy it brings me, I appreciate the joy it must also bring others.

Asking for help gives another person the opportunity to *feel* – and so the beautiful flow of abundance grows.

Amy, 44

Chapter 7

Permission to ask

When I moved to Australia from England, I was six months pregnant with my first child. I had left behind a successful acting career that had allowed me to be financially secure and independent. I had my own flat that I was paying a mortgage on and I had been enjoying the life of a single woman in London.

Then all my circumstances completely changed. I was living in a country I did not know or understand (it is amazing how different Australia is to England), I was living with my in-laws and I was about to become a new mum away from everything and everyone I had ever known.

Then I became a mother, and my feelings of independence slowly began to dwindle. My husband was working for a salary and I was a stay-at-home mum – which was my choice, but which definitely had an impact on how I saw my role as a not-so-independent woman.

As my husband was earning the money, I felt I had to ask him for permission before I spent anything. It felt like I was asking for permission to live my life, which was not a feeling I was used to at all.

He never told me I had to do this – I had unconsciously decided that if he was earning the money, it was his and I needed to ask for permission to spend it.

At that time, I had no idea we were both co-creating the life we wanted to live, equally. I was at home with the children so that he could earn; he was earning so that I could be at home with the children. Neither of us could do what we were doing without the other. I believe many women who find themselves in this situation forget this fact.

But I found myself asking my husband for money – asking for permission to have it. I had created this horrible situation for myself and in my mind I had gone from being a successful independent woman to a disempowered 'mother and wifey'.

Before long I started to resent not just the situation but also my husband. I felt that he had power over me, although I now know that I was giving my power away to him.

Women give their power away all the time. I do not mean the overarching power of domination or control, but our personal power.

Sometimes our 'giveaways' are so small, we do not realise how this is chipping away at our own self-worth.

An exercise in permission and personal power

When I first began coaching I was working with a client who had decided to focus on her own wellbeing as a goal. We were exploring what self-care meant to her so that we could create measurable goals to aim for. After a few sessions I felt it was time to set her a challenge.

As a coach, I will ask permission from a client to set them a challenge, and of course they can accept, refuse or make a counter-offer (more on those later).

I asked her if she was willing to take herself out on a dinner date – a date with herself. She had to ask for the best table in the house, and order for herself whatever she wanted to eat.

She took on the challenge and we agreed that she would share how the experience was for her in our next session.

When we next spoke, she said, 'I did everything we created in the challenge. It was a wonderful night and from now on I will take myself on a date the last Friday of every month. It is going to be part of my regular self-care routine.'

I was very happy for her. It was wonderful that she had enjoyed the experience so much and had already decided how she was going to bring it to her life in a sustainable and measurable way.

But what she said next really moved me.

'Kemi, the biggest gift I got from the date with myself was when I was reading the menu. As I was looking at all the meal options, I realised that I had not chosen a meal for myself in about 30 years.'

I wanted to know more.

'As a child I had to eat whatever was put in front of me,' she said. 'And when I married as a young adult at 18, my husband always chose what we ate, even though I did all the cooking.

'Whenever we went out for a meal with friends or family I never wanted to be a bother,' she continued. 'I hated the thought of holding anyone up. So, instead of taking the time to choose what I wanted to eat, I would always defer to the majority order – what most of the people around the table were ordering – and that way I would not cause a fuss.

'I never knew I did that until the other night when I was on my date with myself.'

I asked her what she had learned about herself from this experience.

'What I know now is that I am worthy enough to have a preference,' she said, 'to have an opinion, to have a choice.'

When I said it sounded like she had given herself permission to ask for what she wanted, she said it was even more than that.

'I have given myself permission to live my life,' she said.

Giving yourself permission

The only person who can give us permission to live the way we want is ourselves.

That means we need to take responsibility for every choice we make, because we are where our personal power lives and everything else stems from this place.

What conversation do you need to have with yourself so that you can give yourself full permission to live? My challenge to you is to grant yourself full permission to ask for what you need, full permission to ask for what you want and full permission to ask for what you desire. Today.

Chapter 8

Our history of asking

I believe that we all have a history when it comes to how we feel about asking. We have all been impacted in some way by what has happened in our lives, and our feelings around asking will generally have come from our childhood.

My own childhood was a complex one with many moves between foster homes.

One of my foster mothers always used to say to me, 'Be grateful for what you have got!' This was never said in a peaceful way that made me more grateful for what I had. It was said with anger and finality. And it never made me feel more grateful – it left me feeling guilty, ashamed and resentful.

When I think about it, that foster mother told me to be grateful for what I had whenever I asked for anything. It was her common response, and it was used as a full stop to any request I made. So in the end I just stopped asking.

As I said, the situation was complex, and I felt that if I rocked the boat too much, I would be moved on to another family. There was no way I wanted to be moved on to family number four, so I stayed quiet.

So that is part of my asking history – asking was not something I was encouraged to do. I was very much in a position where my experience of life was in the hands of others, not to be negotiated in any way.

Every childhood is different, and every child will react in their own way within a given situation. Imagine being a child raised by parents who were always asking for a discount or deals. As a result, you might grow up knowing that asking can support your financial responsibilities and dreams. Or you might feel inferior and embarrassed because of your parents' behaviour, so for you asking is a humiliating sign of weakness.

It all comes down to how you interpreted your early experiences.

Recreating your relationship with asking

Because you may have witnessed or heard many negative messages in regards to asking when you were growing up, your first step to creating a new relationship with asking is to explore your personal history and to understand where the feelings you have now stem from.

'Do not be greedy...', 'Do not rock the boat...', 'Take what you are given!', 'Do not make a scene.'

These are classic responses that may stir up guilt, shame, embarrassment, rejection and fear for you. But there is no right or wrong – learn to be curious about the thoughts and the emotions they trigger.

Once you have accessed these thoughts and emotions, ask yourself if your current relationship to asking is helping or hindering you in your desire to create the life you want for yourself.

Keep in mind that every time we have the courage to ask for what we need, we are creating an opportunity for ourselves. We can create new relationships, new possibilities, better outcomes, more peace, enhanced wellbeing, better communication. We can create new worlds.

Next time you are feeling blocked, overwhelmed or hindered, it may be that your asking history is resurfacing and affecting the way you see and do things. So ask yourself, 'What am I not asking for that is making me feel this way?' And give yourself the wonderful gift of asking. Because in doing so you are not being greedy and you are not rocking the boat. You are entitled to as much as you want and, you know what? If you want to make a scene, go ahead, knock yourself out!

Irina's asking story

I wish I had asked my mum so many questions about her – as a woman, as a little girl, her memories, her experiences, her fears, joys, how she was when she was a teenager, when she became a mother, her dreams.

So many questions I never asked and now it is too late because her mind is gone.

I remember talking to my mum in the kitchen in Chile about my friends, the things we did, the fights we had, about boys. Or we would gossip about the aunties or neighbours, or about her nutcase rich boss.

I would listen to her advice about how to be a proper respectable girl. How I had to honour and respect myself so only good boys would come my way.

But I do not remember asking her any questions.

Now that I am a grown-up woman I am trying to collect all the advice she gave and I am trying to imagine the answer my mum would give me, but it is sad I will never get to hear her real answers.

I do not know why I did not ask her. Maybe because I only saw my mother as my mother – I did not care about my mother as a whole woman.

Now I have to ask questions to my older female friends and learn about womanhood from their experiences.

My mother was my port of departure. The cost of trying to figure out things on my own has left me feeling lost. I am feeling like I am navigating without any point of reference.

If I had asked my mother how she felt in her marriage, how she dealt with money, how she dealt with the pain of seeing her sons suffer, her desolations, her aspirations and her coping mechanisms, I would not feel so lost because I would have her answers.

I think my marriage ended because I did not know how to be a whole woman. I did not know how to find wisdom and strength to sort out all of the differences and difficulties. It all got too much because I was so lost. I needed to free myself to start all over again from a fresh new port and start navigating my own route.

In our mothers and grandmothers lies a treasure of feminine wisdom. I am planning to collect as much information about myself as I can, so I can pass it on to my daughter. When she comes to navigate difficult waters I would like to be a point of reference for her.

I often wonder what my mother's answers would have been if I had asked her about my doubts and queries. I question myself about what would she have done in my situation, but I cannot get her answers because she has dementia and she no longer recognises me.

I wish I had asked her those many questions about her.

Irina, 45

Asking Process #1
Your asking history

Throughout this book you are going to come across five Asking Processes, all of which are geared towards building up your 'asking muscle'.

This first one, Asking Process #1, requires you to go inside yourself rather than do any asking of others.

We need to go internally first to be clear about where we have come from, because this affects how we are now. Once we are aware of this, we can create where we are going and who we will be when we get there.

In the chapters so far I have talked about some of the reasons women in general do not ask, as well as sharing some of the stories from my own asking journey, and you have read the asking stories of Tantalika, Amy and Irina.

Now it is your turn.

You will be amazed at what this process will uncover for you, so carve out some alone time for yourself to allow you to concentrate fully on doing so.

Grab a pen and a journal, if you use one, or a notepad or notebook of some sort, as you will want to capture your answers with your own writing. It is a good idea to dedicate a particular book or notepad to this, as I will be giving you five Asking Processes, and in the remaining four you will need to refer back to what you have written previously.

Create your own asking story

The questions below are very similar to the questions I asked the women, like Tantalika, Amy and Irina, who share their stories throughout *The Gift of Asking*. Answer these questions as well as you can and they will create the framework of your asking story.

- What did you learn about asking as a child? (Think about the good and the bad, or maybe there was nothing.)

- Looking back to your past, what did you never ask for that you wish you had? (Think about work, relationships, family, health, lifestyle and material wants.)

- Why did you not ask? (Explore internal and external factors – things you thought to yourself and what others said.)

- What has been the cost to you of not asking? (Again, think about internal and external factors.)

- Has anyone else been impacted by you not asking, either at the time or since? (Think about your children, colleagues, family and friends.)

- What has been the biggest ask of your life so far? (It might have involved love, money, support, space or maybe an opinion.)

- What have you gained through the process of asking, even if you did not get the specific thing? (It could have been pride, strength, resolve, clarity, a burden lifted, connection, personal power.)

- What have you learned about asking in your life so far?

- Would asking for what you need and want make a difference to you and the way you currently experience life?

This is your asking history

How did you go? This is not a test – whatever came up for you is perfect for you to start working from. Hopefully you now have a clearer idea of what and why you do or do not do in regards to asking for your needs and wants. The power of writing our experiences down always provides the opportunity for reflection, clarity and growth.

Now that you are aware of your history so far, I invite you – in your daily life – to see where it reveals itself. There is nothing specific you need to do about it right now – just be willing to explore and be curious about your new awareness.

Chapter 9
Not asking equals not knowing

Sometimes we choose the pain of not knowing the answer to a vulnerable question – we delude ourselves that there is safety in not knowing, that this is somehow better than the pain and responsibility of knowing the actual answer and being present to the truth of a situation. You know how the saying goes, 'Better the devil you know...'

What kind of questions am I talking about? You know the kind – they make you feel incredibly uncomfortable when you think about them. You get palpitations and anxiety when the subject is broached or someone else is about to ask or answer a similar question. You carefully avoid the asking of them.

These are a few examples, but you will have your own.

Does she love me?

Am I going to be invited to the party?

When will they pay me back the money they owe me?

Am I being a good enough mother/partner/friend?

Am I being a good enough boss?

Generally, we need to know the answer to this kind of question so we can know where we are starting from and what needs to be changed. Sometimes the answer means we have to move on. And moving on will guarantee a certain level of emotional pain and turmoil.

So rather than actually asking the question and facing the music, so to speak, we avoid asking and spend our time making up worst-case scenarios. We expect the worst and we ruminate until it feels like our brain is eating itself.

Well, that is what I used to do.

As human beings we have a need for certainty, and I think sometimes we would rather convince ourselves of the worst-case scenario because it is an outcome of some sort. 'It is all doomed.'

The second option – knowing the answer we need to move forward – only brings pain if we do not get the outcome we are hoping. On the flipside, we may get the answer we were hoping for.

Knowing has more favourable odds, even if you do not get the answer you want, you now have everything you need to decide your next action.

Which pain do you prefer?

The pain of knowing is the emotionally healthier choice, but it can be a hard one to make.

If we do not have the information we need, we are living in limbo – a place where it is impossible to feel empowered. So there is the *definite* pain and suffering of *not* knowing, compared to the *possible* pain and suffering of *knowing*.

If we are to thrive in our lives, we have to be willing to live with emotional pain; it is part of the deal. And it is actually possible to be comfortable in pain and suffering if it leads you to personal power, to growth and to where you want to be.

If we do not know what is happening in a situation – be it in our personal life, at work, in a relationship, in our family – how can we possibly choose what to do next?

If not asking equals not knowing, you have chosen ongoing self-inflicted pain and suffering over the opportunity to be hurt, to recover and to move on.

Anne's asking story

When I give it some thought, up until recently I had been acting based on what I thought people wanted instead of asking actual questions ever since I was a child. At school I would not ask questions because I did not want to be that annoying girl who keeps interrupting the class with more questions. And it was the same at home, I suppose. It is as though being curious or wanting to clear up misunderstandings through asking were not valued as good qualities – they were seen as social flaws.

I felt the same at home. Not that I grew up in an environment where it was not possible to ask, it just felt like I couldn't.

So I never asked about – or asked for – so many things that would have made my life different. I never asked if it was okay to fail or what would happen if I made the wrong choices. I wish I had.

I have never asked my parents what made them fall in love or how I was born. Maybe I should.

I wish I had asked what was expected of me from my parents, my boyfriends, my piano teacher, my managers. I wish I had asked my mum earlier about that yoga thing she was always talking about.

I wish I had asked if there was an alternative to taking the Pill and why it was important to wear my retainer after I got my braces removed. I wish I had asked what made people love me, and what made them feel loved in return. I wish I had asked my grandmother to teach me how to speak Italian and how to sew properly.

When I was employed in corporate jobs, I wish I had asked to be paid for the fair value of the work I was doing. I wish I had asked what success is – and had not based my life on my own twisted version.

I wish I had asked *all* these questions so I would not have created the answers in my mind and taken them for truth.

Why did I not ask? I do not even know now. Maybe because I did not think about it or I did not dare to.

Not asking these questions, and deciding I had to figure it out all on my own, cost me in terms of lost opportunities for more knowledge, better understanding and personal growth. Mostly, though, I regret being trapped by my own answers and the years I spent putting tons of unnecessary pressure on myself trying to fulfil them.

It was me who decided what others were expecting of me and what I had to do to gain their love, trust or pride. Only recently have I understood that these people – my family, my friends, my partners, my colleagues – would never have asked me to push myself the way I did. It was not fair to them, let alone to me.

I was deeply touched when I listened to Kemi's story of being taken shopping by her new foster family and being asked what colour underpants she would like – being given a choice for the first time in her life. And what this story really taught me is that when we ask others, we give them the opportunity to choose their answer instead of making that choice for them.

I also learnt an important lesson about asking from the CEO of the French high-tech company where I worked for seven years. This man is a visionary who likes to be involved in all aspects of his business, and does not care much for company management structures or hierarchies. He likes to talk directly to the person in charge of a particular process – the person he can get real answers from. Of course, in such a big company that is not always possible, and I can remember his response in meetings where he would ask a project manager a very specific question, say, about a modification to a particular element. If that manager started blindly trying to come up with an answer, the CEO would thunder, 'Have you asked the person who looks after that part? No!? Then go and ask them! And then tell me what they say! *Do not make the questions and the answers!*'

Do not make the questions and the answers. That sentence has remained imprinted in my mind ever since because *this is me*. This is what I have been doing for years – not asking, but anticipating the answers.

When you make the questions and the answers, there is no choice, no perspective, no opportunity.

After a breakthrough ask for help – the biggest ask of my life – I now give myself permission to ask more, about anything.

I have asked for help to support my journey as a small business owner in many ways – I have asked for coaching and mentorship; I have asked for money to overcome temporary cash flow issues; I have asked for other people's time to brainstorm ideas and help build projects.

I thought that by asking for help I would feel like a failure, but the strangest thing was I actually felt empowered – from the first moment of asking I felt lighter, more grounded and stronger.

By asking, I gave myself permission to not do it all on my own. And as a result, I got the support I needed and a deepening of valuable relationships, too.

This process has also made me aware that asking is not simply about the question; it is also very much about whom you ask. I have learned that not all of the people around us are the right people to ask for this help; they may be the most loving and caring, but they still may not be the *right* people.

I am 32 years old now and there are probably still things I do not ask for, but now I know that I can. As part of the process I am also learning to ask others what they need from me.

All these questions and their answers nourish me, allow me to grow and eventually to become a better teacher, a better daughter, a better lover, a better friend, a better cook, and so on.

Asking for what I want or need gives me intention. It helps me to own my dreams.

Anne, 32

Chapter 10
Tricky questions we need to ask

In those rare moments when everything in life seems to be humming along nicely, do you start to worry whether something is about to come along and upset the apple cart? Or at those moments are you even tempted – or compelled – to upset the apple cart yourself?

Our experience of life so far is generally what dictates how happy and comfortable we are with things humming along nicely. It can actually be unsettling and disturbing for those of us with a history of trauma when everything is going well – it can feel foreign and therefore scary for us. Which is why we often pull out our trusty tried-and-tested self-sabotage rituals to mess things up.

What has this to do with questions we need to ask? Stay with me and you will see.

In the past when things were going well I used to have a fear that I would have a heart attack.

Being moved around to different foster families as a child was stressful. Just when I felt I had settled in with a new family, when I was starting to feel 'at home', I would be moved. And each time I felt my heart was literally being attacked. Hence the self-inflicted 'heart attack' when things were going well for me in my adult life.

At those times, when all was well with my life, I would plunge from that very fulfilled and happy place to one where I was fearing death and feeling petrified because I would not be able to say goodbye to my children.

Eventually I realised I needed to ask myself a question – and a tricky one at that: 'Can I be okay with being okay?'

Thankfully, an upset apple cart is always an opportunity for growth and the answer to this question came to me after doing my own personal development work. Yes, I am okay with being okay. In fact, these days I am happy with things being better than okay.

Are you?

Keeping your apple cart on its wheels

We are all capable of upsetting our own apple cart and causing personal suffering that leaves us feeling overwhelmed, alone, taken for granted and resentful. Of course, we do not always know we are doing this – it can take a few goes for us to realise we are in a pattern.

Developing awareness of what we are doing and why we are doing it is definitely the first step to transforming any situation. When the realistion does come, or starts to come, the following exercise will give you the opportunity to break some of your patterns.

Asking Process #2
Personal needs

This is the second 'Asking Process' section of *The Gift of Asking*. In the first Asking Process (page 58) I asked you to reflect on your asking history. And now we look at your personal needs.

We all have personal needs. They are a part of our human make-up and we require to have them met to be the best version of ourselves.

It is incredibly important to be honest with yourself about what you need. It is also essential to put aside any assumptions about virtuous needs versus greedy needs (look back to the Introduction of this book on page 3 if you would like to be reminded of what I say about these).

This is where you can put into action for yourself what we have been talking and thinking about in the previous chapters. In this Asking Process, you have the opportunity to list all of the things you feel you need or want to be the best person you can be. So grab a notepad, notebook or whatever you like, to jot things down in or on, and prepare to make a list of 10 things you really need to be the best you.

Here are some of the things I need in my life right now, keeping in mind that they will change as I change:

- Time in nature
- A fulfilling sex life
- Quality time with my children
- To move my body and sweat six days a week
- Inspiring and empowering media
- Fun and adventure

- Fulfilling and meaningful work
- Wonderful food that fuels my body and spirit
- To be around women who elevate and support each other
- To nourish my creative needs

Coming up with 10 things is extremely hard for some women, and it may take you a little time to access the ones buried deep within. On the other hand, you may find 20 needs pop into your head before you know it, but for now just make a list of 10.

I need...
I want...
I desire...

Use whatever words are most comfortable for you and write your list of 10 needs now.

Once you have finished your list, take a moment to check in with yourself and see how you are feeling about owning your needs and desires. Does it feel empowering? Scary? Embarrassing?

Whatever you are feeling is okay. Just acknowledge it. They are your needs – no one else's.

This list will be the road map for your asking journey throughout this book. It may change as you ask for different things, so feel free to add and take away.

It is your life and it is your list. Own it.

Chapter 11
The worthiness test

Let me tell you a story...

A few years back, I had just finished a huge work project and I wanted to acknowledge myself and the work I had done by buying something beautiful for my home. For some time, I had been stalking a particular furniture designer and manufacturer for his eco wood and beautiful design aesthetic, and I had decided that when I had successfully completed this project I would finally splash out on two pieces of his furniture.

This was going to be my first piece of designer furniture – a real treat and a true celebration.

The day I arrived at the showroom I was incredibly excited. I imagined that every time I looked at and used this furniture I would be reminded of the project I had completed, the contribution I had made through my work, of how far I had come as a business and the personal growth I had achieved. It was big.

I asked the sales assistant about the pieces I wanted to buy and he asked if I wanted to have them delivered or to take them home that day.

Then I spied the 'seconds' room.

As I looked over to the far corner, I spotted the pieces I was going to buy but at 30 per cent cheaper. I went over to them and had a closer look – they had deep scratches in them, one was dented and a little of the finish was coming off the other piece.

I stood there not knowing what to do; something was shifting in my thinking.

My mind was giving me all sorts of contradictory messages:

'Of course you have to get the discount pieces – that is what a sensible person would do.'

'You have earned this. Treat yourself.'

'What would your parents do if they knew you were thinking of spending this much money on furniture?'

'Go ahead and get the perfect ones – you deserve them!'

'Either way, this is a ridiculous way to spend your money – what are you thinking?!'

'You have worked really hard and this is a great way to reward yourself.'

'Don't be greedy.'

'Celebrate your success!'

Settling for second best

As it turns out, in that moment I decided that I did not deserve the perfect furniture enough – I had not done enough to earn it and, besides, I had to be responsible.

I felt too guilty and I was unable to give to myself what I really wanted, so I settled for second best and chose the damaged goods.

Not surprisingly, the trip home with the purchases in my car was not the exhilarating journey I had anticipated. I was happy enough to have the pieces, but knowing I had let myself down had taken the edge off the excitement. I had asked myself for a fitting reward and then told myself I was not worth it.

The consequences of unworthy asking

To this day, every time I look at those pieces of furniture I do not think, 'Wow, that was a great achievement! Good on you!'

No, instead I think, 'Great. Another moment when you decided you were not worthy enough to allow yourself to have what you really wanted.'

Another lesson learnt.

The issue was not about the furniture or the price – it was about my sense of self. It was about what I thought I was worth.

We all do that, don't we. Settle for second best.

We think, 'This is good enough. It is not quite what I want, but it will do.'

Of course, making a call to take second best is appropriate from time to time – sometimes good enough is enough and compromise is the best option. But if we find ourselves regularly feeling that we drew the short straw, that our ship did not come in yet again, we have the chance to ask ourselves, 'Is the problem that I actually think I am not worthy of more?'

It is only when we decide we are worth more that we begin to make different choices, and different choices create different actions – the kind that create a new way of living.

Passing the worthiness test

I learnt a great lesson that day, and ever since then I have been able to celebrate my achievements fully.

And as a coach, encouraging my clients to celebrate themselves is part of my work. We so often forget to mark and reward ourselves for what we have achieved, and yet we are worthy of celebration.

Ask yourself: 'Where am I settling for second best?'

And then ask yourself: 'What do I intend to do about it?'

Asking Process #3
Committing to action

Doing this Asking Process allows you to look at the areas in your life that are not thriving, and will bring about clarity around what needs to be asked for and what your barriers to asking may be.

Find your journal, notebook or a notepad, as you did in Asking Process #1 on page 58 and Asking Process #2 on page 71. The process of writing 'from yourself' has the ability to create internal shifts.

To start with, think of or write down three areas of your life where you want improvement. The list that follows is what most women consider to be the most important areas of life. You can use this list to inspire you or just write down your own.

Feel free to use the asking list you wrote when doing Asking Process #2 as a reference, but also be open to something new coming up. What you wanted at the beginning of this book may have changed or it may be even more important now.

If there are more than three areas you would like to work on, just pick the top three priority areas for now – the ones where you could make a real difference at present, or that would have the biggest impact on the other areas. For example, maybe looking after your personal wellbeing will have an impact on your intimate relationship and your fun and creativity.

Areas to thrive in

- Personal wellbeing
- Intimate partner
- Health

77

- Spiritual practice
- Friends and family
- Money
- Creativity, fun and leisure
- Community contribution
- Home environment
- Career
- Passion and purpose

Gaining clarity

Now, starting with the first area, write one sentence to describe what you want. It is important to focus on what you want, not on what you do not want.

For example, *I want my partner and me to reignite the passion and fun in our relationship.*

Now answer the following questions in respect to this sentence:

- To make a difference in this area, who would I need to ask?
- If I were to ask for what I need in one sentence, what would I ask for?
- What are the barriers preventing me from asking?

Repeat the writing down, asking and answering with the two remaining areas.

If you are not ready to ask yet, that is fine; sometimes it is enough to be clear on where your lack of satisfaction is coming from, and it is okay to know what we need to do and not be ready to do it – yet.

But if you want more and you are ready to begin thriving in this area of your life, now is the time to commit to action.

It is easier to carry out an action when it is measurable, and the next question will allow you to create a grounded and measurable goal in this area:

When are you going to ask?

This means being specific and naming a date, a time and a place when and where you are going to ask for what you want.

There is a marked difference between 'I will ask her sometime next week' and 'I will ask her about giving me more responsibility in the project next Wednesday in our 3pm meeting'.

Not some day. Not when you feel like it. But when you are committed to it.

This is when change occurs.

Prue's asking story

Because my mum left me with my dad when I was two and moved overseas for two years, I have blocked many of my early memories. But I do remember my father being quite grumpy and on edge, which made me too scared to ask for anything.

And then they would get back together, fight and break up again, so life was pretty turbulent. I think that because of my parents' mental-health issues, addictions and money problems, I learned never to ask for anything.

All I ever wanted was to go on a picnic and do normal family activities full of joy. I just needed to be loved. But I did not know that, and I did not know how to ask for it.

Asking never worked for me, so I stopped asking and never worked out how to do it properly.

So as an adult myself, I did not use the right techniques when I was asking my partner for help and support. I asked over and over again for small things, which came across to him as nagging. But I never asked for help with the big, important things.

I needed help desperately when I had my daughter – we had just moved to a new city, my dad had passed away the month before and it was the middle of winter – but I did not know how to ask. Having a new baby at home was supposed to be a time filled with love and joy, but I was tired, sad, lonely and too afraid to talk to anyone about how I was feeling.

Instead I suppressed my emotions and just got on with making myself as busy as possible to avoid feeling anything. I wish I had asked for help, but I did not know where to start or where to go, and I was too embarrassed to tell my friends. And I could not rely on my family – I was scared of being yelled at, ignored or let down. I was scared of my mother saying she would help, but not actually do anything.

That insecurity was behind me not asking for more from relationships, I guess. I found it really tough to ask for things. Actually, I did not even know exactly what it was that I wanted or needed from a relationship – not with a lover, friends or family. My low feelings of self-worth really held me back, and because I never felt good enough, I was always thinking about what others might need from me first.

It is so stressful, not being able to ask for what you need. Even though I was falling apart on the inside when my daughter was young, I held up an armour of strength on the outside. And the stress I was under because I was not getting the support I needed really affected my relationship as a mum with my daughter, and also my relationship with her father.

But I am working very hard on breaking the patterns and the cycle of my own childhood by being there for my daughter as much as I can. It feels foreign to me, after not having been loved or shown affection when I was a child. My daughter teaches me more about love and affection than anyone I have ever met. Children are born with an innate nature of pure love.

But there is one place in my life where I have always been confident. I know how to ask for what I deserve in my work and career. I clearly define my goals and whenever I have worked for other people, I have not been afraid to ask for things such as being paid more or flexibility in working hours.

Asking for money in my personal life is not easy for me, though. The biggest thing I have ever asked was to borrow money from my uncle so I could set up a home for my daughter and me when I separated from her father. I had never asked for money from anyone before and I dislike the feeling of being in debt to someone.

I felt so disappointed in myself that I had come to a point in my adult life where I needed to ask for help in this way. I was ashamed that I was in such a bad situation – ending an emotionally volatile relationship, and having no money despite running two businesses that were burning me into the ground, while trying to be a good mum. Having to beg for money was the last straw.

But even though asking did not feel good at the time, it allowed me to find our own place to live in, buy the furniture we needed and to feel safe.

Asking worked for me on that occasion but I am still finding it difficult to ask for the love and support I need from friends and family. So I have been going inwards to find my own pure love and learn to be the best person I can be.

And even though asking is one of the hardest things for me to do, I know when it comes to business, if you do not ask, you will not receive. Also, I have realised people love being asked to help others – it gives them a feeling of purpose.

My life so far has taught me that asking for what you need from others is important. I have also learned that with all of us so busy living our hectic lives, we need to check in with each other. I think if people asked each other how they were coping and if they needed anything more often, there would be less remorse and resentment.

We all – adults, children, everyone – are entitled to ask for love and support when we need it, and to believe we are worthy enough to ask and worthy enough to receive it.

Prue, 33

Chapter 12
Asking out loud

I love to go to the gym. Yes, I am one of the few who do. I have loved the gym from the first time I ever stepped into one at the age of 20, which is 23 years ago.

During this time, I have found myself in many group fitness classes and have always loved the community spirit and fun that can be had when working out with others. Over the past few years there has been more and more hip-hop music added to playlists for its upbeat and aggressive mood that encourages you to 'pump more iron' – to feel invincible and keep going for longer.

But, unfortunately, many hip-hop songs feature the 'N-word', and generally not just once, but again and again and again. (Do an online search for 'the N-word' if you do not know what it is; it will come up for you, I have checked.)

There are many schools of thought about the use of this word. The two dominating opinions are: 1) Africans are claiming back the word to desensitise themselves from the negative implication of it that dates back to slavery; or 2) it is an offensive word that makes many African people feel attacked, and tries to make them ashamed of their heritage.

I fall into the latter category. I was called this name so much at school, and it has been shouted at me from passing cars so much as an adult, that I am incredibly impacted and offended by its use.

Back at the gym, many times I have found myself to be the only black person in my fitness class, and suddenly the 'N-word' is all over the place. It does not make me feel upbeat or invincible; it does the complete opposite.

The first few times this happened I talked myself out of saying anything. I did not want to cause a scene, or be considered oversensitive or a spoil sport for asking the music to be changed. I wanted to be good and not rock the boat.

After a while, though, I felt compelled to say something.

I plucked up the courage – of which it took a lot – and asked the gym instructor if she could change the music as I found it offensive.

She did, straight away, saying, 'I had never even thought about it, but now you have shared that with me, I completely understand.'

I thanked her.

This has happened a few times now, not just in gyms but in cafés as well. Once I was sitting in a local café with my husband and children, and some very hardcore hip hop came on. So I asked – loud enough for everyone to hear – for the song to be changed because of its lyrics. On that occasion they changed the music, but if I ask and the person ever decides they will not change the music, I then get to decide if I want to stay there or not. It is not about what they are 'doing' to me. It is about me asking for what I need, waiting for the answer and then choosing my next action from my own sense of self-worth.

Shaking off the curse of the angry black woman

In Chapter 5 I talked about the 'curse of the good girl' and how it affects a woman's ability to ask for what she needs. Well, being a black woman comes with another set of assumptions – including the ones that mean every time I choose to ask for certain things, I have to wrestle with the question, 'Will people think I am an angry black woman?'

And when I do, I think about the words and actions of former US First Lady Michelle Obama. Tired of attracting the offensive 'angry black woman' label which she explicitly commented on in 2012 after having to address her portrayal in a book by a *New York Times* reporter she thought, 'Okay, well, let me live my life out loud so that people can see and then judge for themselves.'

The thought of being labelled stopped me in my tracks for many years, but now, following Michelle Obama's example, I choose to live out loud instead. What people think is what people choose to think, and none of us has any control over that.

Chapter 13
Your breakthrough ask

We all have limiting beliefs in regards to what we can ask for. Some things we believe we are worthy to ask for, and others not so much.

What would be a breakthrough ask for you?

It could be something you have always wanted, something that has always been denied to you, or something that would change your life because of the joy, relief or validation it would give you.

Don't hold back. This is the ask that will open the floodgates! After all you have read about the gift of asking in the previous chapters of this book, this is the ask that will activate your power for asking for whatever you need from now on.

If you need some help, the list below includes just some of the options we are allowed to ask for.

Here goes.

The Asking Manifesto

You can ask for... more time, an upgrade, more hugs, less chutney, a better rate, more time, a different colour, more intimacy, a different position, more ice-cream, less time, more support, more love, another opinion, a deal, more work, more loyalty, more space, no music, better service, feedback, to change seats, a place in a project, a babysitter, a carer, a tampon, money, clarity, another chance, a holiday, better rules, a way to make a bigger difference, less arguing, more connection, a break, more emotional support, professional advice, more information, more water, the chance to move places to start again, a conversation, commitment, co-operation, more fun, the truth, a thank-you, a loan, a friend, less work, more opportunities, more input, more kisses, more silence, the biggest piece of cake, better resources, a second helping, mentoring, advice, another room, a better outcome, an exchange, more sex, consideration, directions, more options, less options, a massage, a chance, more help, more sleep, a discount, a truce, clarification, an interview, another date, another time, back-up, fidelity, a transfer, a word, respect, more diversity, better odds, a partnership... and so much more.

Remember to download your free resources. They include a beautiful design of The Asking Manifesto.

Go to kemibooks.com to get yours.

Asking Process #4
Start asking now

It is time.

Looking back at the asking lists you have already created in Asking Process #2 and Asking Process #3, what do you consider to be the hardest ask on your lists? Which one makes your stomach flip, your internal voice chatter and a wave of nausea overtake you?

If none of them do, you need a braver list. Go on, get brave!

Now, order and number your list of 10, placing the hardest ask at the top and making it number 1. This is your 'peak ask' – the ask that overshadows all the others on the list.

Now, you are going to start at basecamp and take a small step towards the peak of the mountain – starting with number 10 and working up through 9, 8, 7, etc.

Take that first step and start asking today.

Stay in touch with yourself

When some women start asking they love the feeling of increased self-worth and personal power, and get through their list in no time.

Others, who perhaps have a few big brave asks to action in their list, may need to take it slower.

Either way, we need to remain aware that during a process like this we can create all sorts of upset in our minds and bodies. This is because it involves taking risks – sometimes really big ones – and stepping out of our comfort zone – sometimes a long way out.

Do not be surprised, for example, if on the day you were going to ask your father to begin paying back the money he owes you, a migraine sends you to bed. Or the day you are going to ask that special person out on a date, your back seizes up.

Do not underestimate the mind/body connection and be curiously honest with yourself about what is happening. Because you are reading this book, you must already have a level of self-awareness – so use that sense of yourself to check what is coming up for you during this new experience.

Ready, set, read this first...

I have been through this process with quite a few women, and I have seen how they have approached it and how they have responded to the outcomes. So here are some guidelines I always give women before they start the asking process.

- Ask each ask as you are ready; maybe even before you are ready.
- As you continue to read through these pages, you will gather more tools to action the bigger asks, so trust in the process.
- The gift of asking is not just about the ask; it is also about who we become during the process. It is about taking stock of the outcomes, learning and discovering new possibilities. We may deepen relationships, bring joy to another, let something go, build a bridge. Or it could throw you off course, be an upsetting outcome or challenge the status quo.
- I suggest that you do not action more than one ask each day.
- Take the time to sit with the pre-ask and post-ask feelings. These will reconnect you with your asking story, and your story will change as you take each step towards the peak ask.
- Celebrate yourself for every ask you action. Give yourself a huge pat on the back and cross it off the list.

- If you love to write, record your experiences in words; if that is not your way, take a moment to acknowledge you are moving up the mountain.

Okay, number 10, here you come. Start asking now.

Being accountable

The power of accountability is well known – it is one of the many reasons working with a coach is such a powerful tool.

It is a fact that when someone else in our life knows what we are going to do, we are more likely to do it.

We might want to be self-sufficient and the sort of person who does what we say we are going to do, but most people are not like that – especially when the action is emotionally risky or hard.

So how will you hold yourself accountable to your asking list? Who will you share it with? Who will you ask to hold you accountable?

To be clear, it is not this person's job to check on you every five minutes; you are sharing your commitment and intention to act with them, and that is enough. They do not have to do anything but listen and be accounted to.

As you complete each ask on the list, you may want to let your person of accountability know – or not, that is for you to decide.

You are in charge of your list; you are in charge of your life.

Be kind to yourself.

Keep taking action.

Keep asking.

Chapter 14
Asking to build others

Recently I ran a group coaching series in which the 30 participants needed to create actions for the week, and I challenged them to make one of the actions an 'asking' action.

I shared my experience that we can only go so far with our goals on our own, and to reach the next level, whatever that might be, we have to ask for support.

So everybody took on the challenge and away they went.

The following week we talked about what they had gotten from taking on the asking action challenge.

One woman shared that she had returned home tired from work one night and wanted pasta for dinner. But when she looked in her food cupboard, she saw that she had run out of pasta. Usually she would have dragged herself back out of the house and gone to the shop to buy some, even though she knew that in the next cupboard was pasta that belonged to her flatmate.

But this time – because the possibility of asking was at the forefront of her mind thanks to the asking action – she decided to ask.

She was extremely nervous when she asked her flatmate for the pasta, even though he was more than happy to give her some.

'I would never normally have asked for a food item from a flatmate, and it was really hard for me,' she said, 'but once I had done it, it felt good. He was happy to contribute to me.'

I asked the rest of the group if they would have found it hard to ask for pasta, and about a third of the room put their hands up.

Another participant had created the goal of wanting to be more financially literate so asked a friend who was a chief financial officer (CFO) for coffee with her to share his knowledge about money and financial security.

'He was so happy to share this knowledge with me,' she said. 'It was really exciting.'

Another woman was having furniture moved for her, where she would usually do it herself; another had deepened her relationship with a new partner by asking him if he would like to tell her about his past relationship that had ended very badly.

'He was so moved that I had asked him about this painful part of his past,' she said. 'He had not wanted to tell me anything about it, in case it impacted on our relationship, but the fact that I asked him made him feel like I was willing to be with his past hurt – that I cared. This was a huge moment in our relationship.'

In all of these situations the person asked was empowered and relationships were deepened. Asking others turns out to be mutually beneficial – it helps the asker and builds up the person who is asked.

Always remember that when we ask, we elevate the other person. We are saying to them, 'You are worthy, you make a difference – and I need your support.'

Chapter 15

Owning your needs – a love story

My own asking story is a real lesson in how acknowledging and expressing your needs and asking for what you want can save a situation – for yourself and others.

As a foster child I was raised by six different mothers. The only one of those women I ever remember asking for what she wanted was my birth mother. She was bold and unapologetic in her asking, and it always embarrassed me.

Like for so many of us, the overwhelming theme of my childhood was not about recognising my needs, let alone owning or satisfying them. Quite the opposite. As a child I was told to be quiet, to be good, to be grateful. I was told to not cause a scene, not cause a fuss, not rock the boat, not be greedy. Every day, over and over, I was told to stay in my place.

And as a black girl growing up in a very white world, I had a very particular place in which to stay.

I was so scared that if I didn't stay in my place – if I did express my opinion, which would inevitably upset the people around me – I would be one of those 'bad black girls'. I had been told enough times as a child that although I was black, I was a 'good one', which I later learnt meant that I was being raised properly because I had white parents; but that is a whole other book.

Living like this as a child and young adult, I felt gagged most of the time – and sometimes I still have that feeling come up. I have learned to recognise it and override it, but it still appears. What I know now that I did not know as a child, is that I have as much right as any other person to have needs and wants.

The letter called 'I need...'

I cannot remember exactly the moment I realised my right to need and want, but I was 26 years old at the time and it involved writing a very long letter to my boyfriend – now my husband – about three months into our dating.

We were having a long-distance relationship, with me working in London and him in Australia travelling around on a solo pilgrimage.

He was living this nomadic life on the west coast of Australia so we had set times when we would talk that were dictated by his movements and his ability to find phone coverage. And although I prided myself for being an independent woman, I found myself hanging out for those phone calls – the curse of love that affects even independent women.

My boyfriend always called when he said he would, but I actually found these 'conversations' incredibly frustrating. You see, he was in travelling mode and would talk at length about everything he was doing, rarely asking me about what was happening in my life or talking to me about our relationship.

So although I looked forward desperately to hearing from him, contact usually left me feeling even more lonely and unsatisfied.

And then, gripped by the emotional angst that is our twenties, I decided to do something about it in the form of a letter called 'I need...' that went something like this:

> *I need for us to have better conversations when we speak.*
> *I need to not be so far away from you – this is horrible.*
> *I need you to ask me how I am.*
> *I need to know what is happening with us.*
> *I need to feel that you are interested in me.*
> *I need to hear that you love me.*
> *I need to hear that you miss me.*

There was more, but you get the gist of it.

'Needy' versus expressing your needs

This may sound 'needy' to you but there were things I needed in my relationship that I was not getting, and I gave myself permission to ask for them.

In fact, when I think about it now, this letter was not about making him give me what I needed but about me declaring my needs, which in turn enabled him to choose what he needed. Did he want the exciting challenge of being with a woman who knew her own mind and knew what she wanted?

The outcome of my letter was not what was important to me at the time. I was very, very unhappy in what felt like an impossible situation – if you have ever been in a long-distance relationship you will know what I mean – and what I needed was to be able to say what I wanted.

After writing this letter I did not feel selfish or greedy or needy. I felt empowered. If he chose to end the relationship, at least I had been clear about my love and what I wanted. If he ended the relationship it would be because he felt he could not give me what I needed, and that was okay.

Ownership 101

To be honest, I am not sure what happened directly after that but he and I have been married for nearly two decades so far…

My message to you is that my needs did not drive him away. My needs allowed him to choose what he wanted and allowed me to become clear about what I wanted, too.

It also opened up a conversation about his needs and wants. Win/win.

You are going to feel gagged at some point in your asking; we all do. It may not look the same as mine in terms of being a good black girl, or a lover in need, but you will have your version.

When you are courageous enough to own your needs, you can actually deepen your relationships and allow people to get closer to you.

And those who cannot give you what you need, do not have to become enemies – they can become your biggest teachers. Meeting them has allowed you to access your needs and sharing your needs has allowed you to know your value. Not your value in their eyes but your value to yourself.

Is there a bigger gift than that?

Chapter 16
Stop shoulding, start asking

Fast forward from the 'I need' letter shared in Chapter 15, to when my boyfriend became my husband and we had become parents.

A very different way of life for me, he went off to work every day and I stayed at home to look after our three-month-old baby.

I had moved from England when I was six months pregnant to live with my in-laws, who I did not know, in a country that had more insects than I had ever seen in my life!

To say I was feeling overwhelmed, vulnerable and out of place is an understatement.

As happens when you are feeding a three-month-old baby four, five, six or however many times a day, you can become fixated on things. When it is just you and a baby, without other mental stimulation, you start noticing things that were not as significant previously.

My eyes went to the carpet. And after dwelling on the state of the carpet for several days, I started wondering why my husband had not noticed the need for cleaning it. Which led me to wondering why he was not coming home from work, picking up the vacuum cleaner and cleaning that carpet.

Next, I started making hints about the carpet – which, of course, is not the ideal clean communication style that would have been preferable, and predictably it had no effect.

Then one morning as my husband was leaving the house to go to work, and I was facing another day of looking at *that* carpet, I exploded at him: 'I cannot believe that you have not seen how dirty the carpet is!'

He stopped in his tracks, looked at the carpet, then at me, and stared blankly.

'Why is it you never see when the place needs tidying up?' I said.

His answer was gold. My husband looked me sincerely in the eye and said, 'I will never see when the carpet needs to be vacuumed. But when you see it needs to be done, just ask me and I will do it, no problem.'

Unfortunately, I did not appreciate the perfection of his reply at the time – hindsight is such a beautiful thing – and I came back with, 'Why should I have to tell you? You live here too! You should see it too!'

He went off to work and I stayed at home and fumed.

Beware your expectations

It took me about a week to realise where I had gone wrong in this exchange. My husband had been very willing to do the vacuuming – he had no problem doing it at all – he would just never see the need to do it at the same level that I did.

My expectation (that he would be interested in having a tidy home to the same extent as me) was completely out of sync with his reality (where he was more focused on our new life in terms of caring for our baby and earning the money to support us).

My husband and I were living our life together but with different priorities and perspectives. And that is why clear and clean communication – including asking instead of hinting and not making 'should' statements after the fact – are what is needed in situations like these.

I had asked him for what I needed, but not in a clean way. He clearly told me how he could give me what I needed, and I refused it because I had an expectation. He had clearly told me he could not fulfil that expectation and gave me a counter-offer. But I was stuck in the view that he *should* know, that he *should* see it. I expected that I *should* not have to tell him.

Confusing? Unclear? Exactly.

So after this debacle I eventually understood my mistake and saw the opportunity I had missed, and I started asking. And my husband started doing.

Reinventing your expectations

What you think someone *should* do is an expectation – your expectation. They will not necessarily see it your way and they are entitled to do what they want or need to do, regardless of what you expect they should do.

The word 'should' is generally not a word we use when we are being kind to ourselves or others. Using 'should' is a sure sign that we have a preconceived idea that something is wrong. This means we are making ourselves and others wrong.

Quite often we have expectations of others without even knowing it, until the particular need is not being met for us and 'should' statements start entering our minds. Before that should statement leaves your mouth, reconfigure/restate/reinvent it so you are asking – clearly and succinctly and from a place where there is no expectation – not 'shoulding'.

Our 'asks' may not always be granted to us in the way we want, but that does not mean they cannot be granted to us in a way that suits the giver. We just need to have the humility to change our expectation of how the gift *should* look.

As the saying goes: 'Do not "should" all over yourself.' And, I would like to add, do not 'should' over anyone else, either.

Sabrina's asking story

I found that as a child asking was an inconvenience – it caused anxiety and stress.

As an adult I will ask on behalf of my daughter – that is not an issue at all. But I have a real problem asking anyone for anything that is to do with me.

I have a friend who is always saying to me, 'Why don't you just ask for help?'

If I am sick and I need someone to take my daughter to school, I find it too hard to ask for myself, so I will take her to school regardless of how sick I am.

I know people who will help, it is just that I cannot ask. I feel it is a total inconvenience to ask them, and I find it stressful.

And my daughter is impacted by me not asking, I know that.

But I have made one big ask. A huge ask. The biggest ask for me in my whole life.

I grew up in the UK, and while I was still living there in London, I asked my brother to go for a walk with me.

You see, when we were young he sexually abused me for many years. His abuse was my first sexual experience. And I asked him to go for a walk in the park to talk to him about that.

I knew that if he said yes to that ask, I would have to go through with it. There was no turning back.

I had to have this conversation because I had met a man whom I thought wanted to marry me, and I knew that if I did not get it resolved with my brother, our marriage was never going to work.

My brother said yes to the walk.

And I was so surprised by what happened next, because he turned around and said to me, 'It is not as if I have not thought about it every day of my life.'

I was totally gob-smacked by this.

Here is a guy who is a heroin addict, who was in and out of prison, and what he had done to me had made a huge impact on him, and that shocked me.

I had never considered that he had thought about it. I had never thought he had felt any remorse.

Learning that he had remorse made me feel free. I finally had freedom.

My second biggest ask is related to when I was working in a café as a waitress and I stole around £3000. I was eventually found out and they asked me to leave.

That sat with me for many, many years.

About 10 years later I managed to track down the café owner I'd stolen the money from. Although I did not really have the money to pay him, I had to contact him and tell him I was sorry.

I just asked his secretary if I could speak to him. Once again, I knew that if I got a yes, there was no turning back.

I did not ask for forgiveness. What we agreed was that I would pay half the money back and he would donate all of this money to a charity of my choice.

The outcome of asking is not as scary as you imagine it to be. My whole imagination about asking my brother and the café owner was horrible. The pre-asking was a nightmare, but the actual end result gave me relief and freedom.

Sabrina, 49

Chapter 17

Intention is important

Asking is not about getting what you want regardless of the needs of anyone else. Nor is it about your needs being more important than another person's needs.

Neither is it about power plays, or dominating, controlling, manipulating, blackmailing, shaming or judging someone else.

Our asking is always better when it comes from a place of personal empowerment, not at the expense of another.

Our asking is also better when it empowers another person, but not at the expense of yourself.

A balancing act

Finding the balance can be difficult, but it is possible for us to receive what we need or want without causing deep upset to another person.

It takes communication skills, it takes practice and sometimes it takes making the other person's feelings as important as your own; it also takes being flexible and it takes grace.

None of these skills can be learned overnight, but the balance can be found.

Keep the intention

Sometimes you will fail at asking effectively, or not be able to avoid hurting others in the process; at other times you will succeed wildly at asking and receiving, with empowerment for others as a positive side effect. But your intention needs to be consistent no matter what.

Your intention comes from the best place when you experience yourself as equally worthy as anyone else. Use it in pursuit of the most fulfilling and on-purpose life that you can, and use it for yourself and all the other people that touch your life.

This intention will attract the many gifts asking can bring to you and others.

Always be kind in your asking. Always do it with grace. Always be grateful, whatever the outcome.

Chapter 18
Asking like a child

Okay, so when I suggest we ask for what we want like a child, I do not mean in a cutesy little voice or screaming out demands during a tantrum; I mean asking again and again and again, like a child does.

As adults there are certain situations where we do ask for something again and again and again – if you are a parent, you may ask your child to please tidy their room more often than you would like to, over and over again; as a member of a sports team you will ask for the ball to be passed to you again and again and again. Sometimes you will get it, sometimes you will not.

But there are some things that for some reason we will only ask for once. It might be a job promotion, or to invite someone special to do something with you.

For women especially, 'I am only going to ask this once...' is a common expression (I have definitely found myself saying it on many an occasion). And saying it is a surefire way of setting yourself up to fail at getting what you really want.

If at first you do not succeed...

Young children have no fear around asking. They will ask for ice-cream again and again and again, and just keep asking until they get some. And if they do not get what they want, they generally just move on to asking for the next thing.

As adults we do not allow ourselves such freedom. Our ego, pride and fear constantly stop us from asking a second time for what we need and want. (And just to let you know, I personally see ice-cream as a need that deserves repeated asking.)

If you ask for a promotion at work and find yourself being passed over, you can just stop there. You wanted a promotion. You did not get it. Chapter finished.

Or you can keep asking.

You can ask for feedback: 'Why was I not promoted this time?'

With that feedback, you can then ask: 'What would I have to work on to be promoted next time?'

And with that feedback you get the opportunity to choose: 'Am I willing to do what it is going to take to get what I want?'

If you do not get the answer you want or need the first time, do not retreat. Think on it and ask again – maybe in a different way, maybe ask someone else, but explore like a child and keep asking.

Chapter 19
Clear and clean asking

It is incredibly important to be clear and clean when you are asking for something.

First of all, this way of communicating increases the chance that you will receive what you want; secondly, it allows the other person – the 'askee' – to give you their answer from a place of clarity.

I am a big believer in clean communication, no matter what the situation, as it gives power to both parties.

Ways of asking to avoid

What we do not want to do is ask with any 'fuzziness' or hidden agendas – no passive aggressive asking, frustrated asking, angry asking, power-play asking, hinting asking, victim asking, asking as a test or asking to shame.

It can be hard to avoid falling into the trap of asking from such places, and sometimes we may not even know we are doing it. But we are more likely to use these kinds of tactics to get what we want when we are in any kind of emotionally charged state.

Is it a win if it is not won fairly? You may end up getting what you asked for, but you will probably be left feeling uneasy about it. And the other person will be left feeling like they have just lost something, maybe something they did not want to give.

Here are some examples of what asking from a negatively triggered emotional place may look like.

Passive-aggressive asking
'Do you think I care how long we go for if you are going to be on your phone the whole time?!'

Frustrated asking
'How many times do I have to ask you to tidy your room?! How many times?!'

Angry asking
'Are you telling me that my budget report is less important than your family?!'

Power-play asking
'As the one who earns the most money, I think I should choose where we go for our holiday. Don't you agree?'

Hinting asking
'That sounds like a really fantastic event. I could be free that day...'

Victim asking

'I suppose that if I come to the wedding you will expect me to take care of the children.'

Asking as a test

'If you loved me you would not go to your brother's place this afternoon – you would stay with me.'

Asking to shame

'Let me ask you a question. Did you really think I would actually like that?'

We are all human and we do not always get it right, but it is important to take the time to be clear about what you are asking for, how you are asking for it and the intention behind your asking.

Michelle G's asking story

Before this episode with a former partner, I wouldn't have said I had a problem with asking. But in hindsight I see that I did – and that my asking issues were about not communicating cleanly and clearly.

I had been seeing this man for a couple of months when he started staying at my place a few nights a week. He wasn't that long out of his previous relationship and had partial custody of his two children.

Before I knew it, those few nights turned into every night. And then I found out he'd been asked to leave the place where he had been living.

Trying to be a good friend – a good girlfriend, I suppose – I decided in my head that I'd let him stay a few weeks, just until he got on his feet, then ask him what his plans were. At the time I felt horrible. I felt like I wasn't being supportive or loving, but I knew I wasn't ready for us to move in together.

I didn't ask him to move out at that point because he'd come to me for help and I felt like I was turning my back on him in his hour of need. I felt so awful even contemplating having to ask him to find his own place, so I tried to do it kindly and gently. And subtly. Too subtly, I realise now.

Another of his friends offered for him to stay with them, so I gently suggested he might stay there a couple of nights a week instead of at my place the whole time – only because we had just started seeing each other, and I needed a bit of space.

That lasted one visit.

So when the subtle approach didn't work, and when the opportunity arose, I decided I'd step it up and be a little more proactive and give him a solution (my usual approach to solving problems). I mentioned that a friend had two spare rooms for rent – perfect for him and his kids, it was out near their schools and sporting clubs, and it was a house with a backyard. I even went out and took photos for him.

But he just ignored the whole thing. And he stayed at my place.

I wanted to be supportive. I wanted to help. I didn't want to be the bad guy. I didn't want to feel guilty and, most of all, I didn't want conflict. But when he ignored my solution, I knew I had to be more direct, which was incredibly difficult for me.

I finally asked him plainly to move out. And he plainly told me, although sounding embarrassed and broken, that he couldn't afford to move out and he had nowhere else to go.

It had taken me a lot of courage to ask him directly to find somewhere else to live. I never would have guessed he'd answer the way he did and not offer any solutions. He just left his response hanging in the air for me to deal with.

I was at a complete loss.

Incredibly, this situation continued for over two years, with his children coming to stay for their visits with him as well. I became increasingly resentful and stressed as time went on. I was in a place I didn't want to be with a very manipulative and controlling man.

Eventually, after just over two years, four of my close friends intervened – independently of each other, which still amazes me – and gave me the reality check I needed to summon the strength to finally ask him to move out.

This was a huge ask for me. I look back now and wish I had been more direct and asked much sooner – if only I had done it before I had gotten in too deep and started to undermine myself. I also wish I had been stronger, been a quick-thinker and stood my ground. I knew what was right for me – what I wanted – but I caved in. Like my mum used to when I was growing up, I became the peacekeeper.

And the cost to me for not asking earlier was feeling pretty miserable for two years or so.

Plus, I didn't realise it at the time, but other people were also impacted by me not asking him to move out. It caused a lot of worry for people I love dearly, and that's the last thing I would ever have wanted to happen.

My amazing friends watched me retreat from their lives and decline mentally, emotionally and physically over the years I was with him. As one of them said at the time, 'I'm watching you lose your spark and it's killing me. I feel so helpless.'

Then there was also the cost to his two children, the innocents in all of this. I had worked hard to make my home their home-away-from-home for two years. And when I asked their father to move out, he never allowed them to return or say goodbye to me or the friends they had made.

But while there was a cost, there was also a return. From that particular situation I've gained a heightened awareness of the need to ask for what you want. Don't wait – be courageous, be honest, be kind, but ask for what you want. Life is short and you don't want to miss out on living it at your best; whether you need to ask for a pay rise, a promotion, a job, help from friends, an invitation to an event or, in my case, getting back my home, my health and my wellbeing.

Sometimes I still feel scared, anxious and intimidated when I'm asking for something I want – but I do it anyway. I remind myself that I've got more to gain than lose; what's a bit of discomfort, embarrassment, rejection or a dent to the ego when the potential payoff is so great!

I also keep in mind that most people are usually more than happy to support you if they can, rather than consciously and maliciously hinder you or make you feel inferior.

I have learned there is no harm in asking – after all, there's a 50 per cent chance you'll get the response you want.

And I've also discovered that the more you ask, the easier it gets – they do say practice makes perfect.

I've noticed that sometimes my asking is spontaneous, straight off the cuff, unplanned, uncensored and it's done before I can think about it. Other times, though, I think it through more.

I'm also learning to listen to my gut more and more, and to take action quickly before I let doubt and insecurity creep in.

These days getting a no response doesn't feel so negative anymore. A no isn't so much a no – it's a not yet or, possibly, this isn't actually quite right for you.

And when I'm the one who is asked, I've noticed that sometimes I'm flattered and sometimes I'm in awe of the cheekiness/courage/ ingenuity of the person asking, but very rarely am I offended or affronted or do I think worse of the person for asking.

Sometimes I say yes or, after giving the ask some thought, sometimes I'm simply unable to facilitate and I say so.

I'm not saying that I find asking easy to do. It's still challenging for me to ask for many things. I'm 45 now, and I'm finding I'm becoming braver and bolder as I get older, and I know that's coming from experience.

I've been thinking about the big asks versus the little asks, too, and I've come to realise that it's not always about the big asks – all asks deserve to be recognised and celebrated. The small asks build confidence to make the big asks. The small asks may also culminate in putting you in the right place to make a big ask.

I also try to remind myself that if you don't ask, you don't get. And that an unexpected response to an ask isn't the end of the story. There could be another opportunity or path that needs to be looked at and explored.

So will asking change my life? It already has and I know it will in the future!

Michelle G, 45

Asking Process #5
Add more

How are you going with the asking list you would have started back at page 77 in Asking Process #3? How many steps up the 10-question mountain have you taken? Are you anywhere near the peak?

Through asking, taking action, and the reflection that has occurred in response to that list, what are you learning about yourself and the way you communicate with others?

What are you learning about the generosity of people?

What are you experiencing in regards to your worthiness?

How is your level of personal power?

Of course, you will only be able to answer these questions if you are taking action. So if that is not the case for you, turn back to page 71 and write your first 10 asks now. Believe me, it is never too late to start exercising your worthiness. If you are waiting to be ready, you may have a long wait.

Start with simple asks to get warmed up. Ask for no avocado when you order your salad for lunch today. Or go really crazy and ask to exchange the avocado for an egg. Ask for a seat on the bus, or ask if someone can move their head so you can see. Start where you can start. Then start.

If you have acted on your asks...

Now, if you have been taking steps up the asking mountain and the peak is in sight, you will be a different woman. How do I know this? Because no one climbs a mountain and remains the same.

And so it is time to add another 10 asking actions to your list. Go ahead. Do not be shy.

You have read quite a few chapters and women's asking stories since you made that first list, all of which may have exposed other needs and wants you have not asked for. If so, add them to your list.

You may even feel like adding the things that you never, ever, ever, imagined you would ask for. Ever.

Marriage. Divorce. A raise. Less work. A clean slate. A second helping.

Then as you continue to read this book, keep adding to your list. And as you live your life, keep adding to this list.

Of course, you may not always be writing your asks down because, in time, you may find yourself in the habit of asking for what you need and want as second nature.

Each time you reach the peak of your asks, a whole new world will open up to you.

And the bigger the mountain, the better the view.

Keep working on that self-worth, too, and own your wants and needs. Because no one can give you what you cannot give to yourself.

Chapter 20
You are not asking for blood

Relax.

Take a breath.

Be brave.

Dive in.

You are only making a request; you are not asking for blood (unless, of course, you actually need blood, in which case you should go ahead and ask for it).

You may get a no, but you can handle a no. You have handled no before.

You may be rejected, but you can handle being rejected. You have handled being rejected before.

You may feel vulnerable, but you can handle being vulnerable. You have been vulnerable before.

There is nothing anyone can tell you in response to a request that will cause your world to collapse forever.

If you do not get the answer you were hoping for, you may have to lick your wounds. You may have to grieve. You may feel embarrassed. You may have to create a plan B. You may have to completely reassess what you thought was important to you. You may have to evaluate all over again how you want to live your life. You may question who you want to spend time with, and you may need to rethink how you want to contribute to the world.

But, ultimately, until you ask, how do you know?

You have everything you need to ask for anything.

Now is your time to rewrite your asking story.

Michelle C's asking story

During my childhood I saw my mother ask for a lot of things and never get them – from asking my father to stop drinking, to asking for fences to be put up on our property, to asking to buy furniture. So, eventually, she stopped asking and if it was within her power, she just went ahead and did it herself.

So that was the big lesson I took from childhood – there really isn't any point in asking for what you want. If you want something, *you* make it happen. If *you* don't make it happen, it most likely won't.

Having decided long ago that I would never rely on anyone else to provide me with what I want, I was actually putting restrictions on myself. I was limiting myself to what I could do singlehandedly, then knocking myself out doing the work of two or three people, and then beating myself up when I couldn't achieve the impossible.

My other rule was that I would not hold anyone else back from having what they wanted.

Interestingly, I married a man who will give me whatever I want, when I want it, if it is within his power. Which sounds wonderful, but often it is at his own expense. When I see this pattern playing out I always pull him up on it. Getting what I want isn't about him not getting what he wants (or anyone else, for that matter). It's about working as a team to both get the things we want or need.

For me, letting people know what I want or need is about honesty. There is the old saying that knowledge is power, but I think knowledge is more about being empowered. So I'm not worried about asking for what I want (putting it out to the universe, as it were), because how else will I achieve what I want?

Equally, I'm not concerned if I don't always get what I want. I'm quite philosophical about that. I believe that it's important to live in harmony with those around us and in that I am more than happy to help others achieve the things they want, just as I am about achieving the things I want.

For me, it's all about mobilising energy to work towards the life I want to have, and the first step is putting the desire out into the world and seeing what comes back.

And this is sometimes uncomfortable. Recently I made some changes to a book I just wrote and sent them to my editor. I made the changes at the stage in the publishing process where, according to the usual process, I'm not supposed to make them. But as I was reading through the book, I realised that it could be better.

I hummed and hawed about making the larger changes before sending them off to my editor because I knew how big a deal this would be for her. In the end I did it because I felt like I would lose nothing in asking, and potentially a lot in not asking.

That was two days ago and I haven't heard back yet about whether the changes can go through. Whenever I think about it I feel a bit sick in my stomach because I am putting my editor out and being a pain in the backside. What if she finds me too difficult to work with and doesn't want any more books from me? But then I just shrug.

There are lessons to be learned from this experience and I know I will be better off from having faced the situation than wondering 'What if?'. No matter which way it turns out. (PS. The changes to my book went through, so I was happy I asked!)

Michelle C, 48

Chapter 21
When the answer is no

Asking will generally invite one of three responses: yes, no or maybe. We have to accept this reality and prepare for a possible no answer when we ask – that is the nature of asking. But even though a no answer can seem like a clear-cut, black-and-white response, if you receive a no the first time you ask for something, there is always a way to build on and navigate that no. These are questions you can ask to explore the possibilities after a no response.

What are your concerns about saying yes?

Sometimes people will tell us no because they have concerns about the outcome of saying yes.

If we are courageous enough to ask in the first place, we are also courageous enough to ask the next question: '*What are your concerns about saying yes to me?*'

The answer to this question will give you a better understanding of what you can do if you want to try for a yes again. It also allows the other person the opportunity to explore their concerns with you, which can be a gift.

Can I make a counter-offer?

A no answer does not have to be the end of the request – you can make a counter-offer. The art of good communication and negotiation involves pre-thinking alternative options you would be happy with, and which the person you are asking would find attractive and reasonable.

For example, you have asked to work a four-day week so that you can manage the other responsibilities in your life. Your boss says no to that request, but rather than accept that as the final answer, you can present a counter-offer:

'What would you need from me so that I could work four days a week?'

'Would you consider me working a four-day week every fortnight or once a month?'

'Would you be open to me working shorter days instead?'

There are always more options if you are willing to ask more questions, but make sure that the counter-offer remains within the boundaries of your need. There is no point in creating a counter-offer that does not actually address your needs.

Is it a forever no or just a no for right now?

A past coaching client had just split up from her partner and found herself in that horrible limbo land where she was not quite sure if the relationship was truly over or if a reconciliation was possible.

In one of our sessions she was sharing with me the sadness and upset she was feeling in this place of not knowing. So when the opportunity came for her to commit to an action related to the session, she decided she would ask her partner to clarify the situation.

She was scared of what the answer might be, but she felt she had to ask. She asked him, 'Are we a no forever or a no for right now?'

He answered that it was a no forever and, of course, she was devastated, but she also experienced a sense of relief. Now that she knew the situation for what it was she could actually grieve and, when she was ready, she could move on.

What would it take for you to say yes?

This question can reveal the conscious or subconscious reasons for the other person's no response, and gives you a chance to tick any boxes they need or want ticked.

Once they have told you what they need from you for their answer to be yes, you can decide if it is worth your time, effort or focus.

Your neighbour may say, 'I am happy to cut down the tree that is blocking your light, and it would be great if you could keep your dog inside in the daylight hours if it is going to bark all day.'

This in turn becomes a chance to ask yourself, 'How much do I want this?' and 'Am I willing to do this to get a yes?'

Do you know of anyone else who might be able to help me?

One of the best pieces of advice I have ever been given goes like this: 'A no can be the beginning of a journey to find the right yes.'

Whenever I am told no, which happens often because I ask a lot, I will ask if the person can suggest someone else who might help, support or partner with me. This has led to many amazing connections and opportunities.

When we stop at the first no, we may be cutting off all sorts of possible weird and wonderful encounters. We must remain open to getting a yes from someone else.

Be grateful – even for a no

When the person we ask takes the time to consider our request, it is important that we always remain thankful – even if the response we get is not what we wanted or expected.

Other people have the right to say no. We have the right to say no, it is part of our personal freedom. But a no is not always intended to be personal. And the ball returns to our end of the court – we still get to choose what we do next.

If you receive a no, you may need to dust yourself off. But once you have done that, you can choose the lesson you want to learn from the experience and then move on to the next action – always getting closer to who you want to be in this world.

Chapter 22
The gift of allowing

Sometimes we do not need to ask for support or help because it is offered. Are you able to allow support when it comes your way? Do you find yourself saying things like:

> *'No, no, no I couldn't possibly accept.'*
> *'No, I'm fine, really.'*
> *'No, it will not be for long.'*
> *'I will just put up with it for now.'*
> *'I am hoping it will change soon...'*

None of these responses to an offer of support honour you or the person who has offered.

When we decline someone else's offer of support, we are declining a part of their humanity, their sense of purpose and their sense of self. We miss the chance to elevate and validate them.

If you need the money, the childcare, the time, the discount, take it.

Trust that the person who is offering you help, is offering because they want to. No one has put them up to it. It is not a trick. They do not want something in return. You will not 'pay' for it later.

If you know this person well and they have a history of over-committing, then invite them to read the previous chapter so they can learn to say no.

But if this person offers to contribute to your life in some way and you need that contribution, please say yes.

Believe that in that moment you are both worthy, and give yourself the opportunity to be generous to two people – yourself and the person who has offered.

Say, 'Yes.'

Chapter 23
When you are the askee

No book about women asking for what we need and want would be complete without a discussion of what to do when we are the 'askees' – the ones being asked.

Many women's default when being asked to do something for someone else is usually to say yes, regardless of whether they have the interest, time or energy to do what has been asked of them.

We are allowed to say no. Saying no doesn't make us mean or unkind – in fact, saying no can be the kindest response for you and the asker.

It is unrealistic to believe that we can be and do everything for everyone. I know that many women try to, but it does not serve them or the people they are trying to serve.

Just as we can expect people to say no to us, we are allowed to say no to others.

Sometimes, even if you *could* say yes, you are not going to *want* to say yes to some people, simply because you do not feel a connection with the asker. And there will be times when you ask, and the askee does not feel connected to you.

It is an important realisation that not everyone is going to like us or connect with who we are, in exactly the same way that we do not like or connect with everyone either. It is normal and natural to not resonate or connect with everyone we meet, and accepting this is powerful.

The consequences of saying no

When I first started saying no it felt like a subversive action. Maybe it was. Being able to say no actually allowed me to have cleaner and more honest communication with those around me. When some women start asking, they get hooked on the feeling and power through their list in no time.

Saying no allowed me to keep focused on the most important and treasured projects and responsibilities – on making the difference I wanted to make in the world as a woman, as a mother and as a member of my immediate and global community.

And when I am focused on these important things, I am better at doing them.

The sky will not fall

Like many women, I used to operate under the delusion that if I did not take on the project or run the workshop or be available to make something happen for someone, then it just would not happen and the sky would most probably fall.

So, one of the things I had to face – that my ego had to face – was that I was not that special in the long run. I realised very early on that if I said no to someone's request, they would very quickly find someone else to do the job.

When I think about it, never in my life has someone said to me, 'Unless you do this, it is not going to happen,' without it being a case of clear-cut emotional blackmail. People have said this to make me feel guilty about saying no, but it has never been actually true. It has always turned out that if it was important, the 'thing' did happen without my involvement.

When people need to find someone to do something, they find someone; that someone does not have to be you.

Be wary of being seduced

People may use flattery, misrepresent a situation, or find and hit you in your soft spot to get what they want from you. And that is when your self-preservation detectors and your ability to say no need to kick in automatically and firmly.

In my case, I have to thank my incredible coach Belinda for helping me find clarity in a situation where I had said yes to a project that ended up not going well.

It was in the days of my previous business, Kemi's Raw Kitchen, and when I was first approached by this woman to be featured in a book that was being launched globally from the US, my gut instinct was to say no. So I thanked her for thinking of me, but said that I would not be participating.

Then she said, 'But you are one of the few women of colour with a profile in the raw food movement and I think it is important for you to be a role model.'

She had me.

And what ensued over the next couple of years was a pretty unpleasant experience. The project itself ended up being badly managed by the author's team. There were insider politics, betrayal and contract issues, and after a very long and drawn-out process I am not sure if the book was ever released. What I do know is it was an ordeal for the author and for me as a contributor.

In her usual masterful way, my coach Belinda summed up the situation perfectly in three words: 'She seduced you.'

'You are committed to women of colour being seen, heard and valued,' Belinda said. 'This matters to you deeply, so even though your instinct was to not get involved, you were seduced by what matters to you.'

She was right – I was seduced, and this became a powerful lesson for me. It is also an issue I find that comes up with my clients, time and time again. It is a very powerful personal trigger to be aware of.

What would seduce you into going against your gut in this way? It could be money, status or, as it is in many cases, the opportunity to 'contribute' to a charitable cause – after all, the idea of 'being good' is incredibly seductive for many women.

Saying no without guilt or apology

You do not have to cause upset or devastation in saying no – there are ways to do it that will leave the other person feeling whole and valued. Consider the following approaches next time you need to navigate your no without harm or hurt.

Defer
Ask to be asked again at a later time.

Elevate

Suggest someone else who you truly believe would love to do the job.

Take time

Do not say yes on the spot. Take the time to look at your calendar realistically, consider your other commitments, and weigh up whether it is important or relevant for you to say yes.

Provide a counter-offer

'I cannot make meringues as I cannot commit that amount of time, but I can bring a fruit plate – would that help?'

Be honest

'Thank you for thinking of me but I am already committed to a few things at the moment and I want to do my best with those.'

When you start saying no, you will be amazed at how the world keeps turning – you will still have friends, you will still have a job, plus you will have more space to say yes to what really matters to you.

And, remember, if it is important to them, the person who asked will find someone else – someone who would be honoured to be asked.

Beware the glasshouse

I think we also need to look at the other side of the equation – when we are the ones who have 'guilted', shamed, demanded, manipulated or emotionally blackmailed someone into doing something.

We have all done it. Some of us may be masters at it.

But how do we feel when the person we have been pressuring eventually says yes? Sometimes we feel we then have to overcompensate and 'make it up' to them, because we feel their resentment

The first rule in all asking is to be clean.

Clean communication is key

I know I have mentioned this several times already, but clean communication is a potent tool worthy of mastering. When we communicate cleanly with others, we get the same respect in return.

And when I say clean, I do not mean harsh, cruel or cold – just clean. We need to state exactly what it is that we want or need without any hidden agendas or tests, then we need to give the other person space to choose and then we need to respect this choice.

The new heroine

If you are asking another women and she declines your ask, acknowledge her for being clear on what she is or is not committed to in her life. You can thank her for setting boundaries for herself, and tell her she inspires you to do the same. You can thank her for considering your ask in the first place.

As women we need to support each other in setting boundaries. We need to see it as a strength. It does not make a woman a bad person when she says no to you or to anyone else. It does not give us the right to judge or demean her.

It is a real gift to come face to face with a woman who knows what she has to give, to whom she wants to give it to, and when. A woman who means to be fully present, 100 per cent committed and totally fulfilled in everything she says yes to.

I think this woman is the new heroine of our times, and you can be her.

Chapter 24

The ultimate question

As women we are pulled in so many different directions all at once, it can be hard to stay centered and grounded.

I was talking to another writer the other day about the idea of 'busy-ness' – of being busy – and she shared something she remembered me saying when we first met.

As she tells it, my response when she asked whether I was very busy was, 'I don't do busy.'

It was the first time she had ever heard anyone say that.

Being grounded, not busy

When I said I don't do busy I meant that everything I do is grounded in what is important for me and my life.

I live a full life, but it is by my own design. My life does not make me feel flustered or rudderless. Of course, if I am involved in a big project, either in my business or in my personal life, the stakes can become very high. I feel it, but I have ways and tools to ground me.

I never feel busy, but if I do not prioritise what is important, I can begin to feel overwhelmed. And when I feel overwhelmed, I am useless to myself and to everyone around me. And then it is time to ask the ultimate question…

Asking *the* question

There is one question I ask myself in these moments that will always bring me back to what is important to me. And because it always has such a profound impact on me, I have started asking my clients the same question, and they find it incredibly helpful too.

I call it the ultimate question because it cuts through the fog, the busy, the overwhelm and can bring us into personal power instantly.

The question is: *'What do I need right now?'*

Sometimes the answer to this question is small – I need to get some fresh air or I need to go to bed early tonight.

But sometimes this question can bring up bigger answers and require bigger actions to be taken – I need to leave my job or end my relationship, I need to drop one of my projects, I need a loan, I need to move, I need to commit.

One of the incredible things about this question – this ask – is that we never know the answer until we ask it. Sometimes the answer will surprise us, sometimes it will scare us and sometimes it will allow us to simply exhale for a moment.

Once you have the answer, though, it again falls into your hands to give yourself what you need – whether you can give it to yourself or ask for it from someone else.

The ultimate gift to others

As I mentioned before, the ultimate question is also a very generous gift you can give to others.

If something works for you there is a very strong chance it will work for other people as well, and I cannot think of anyone who would not benefit from being asked this question every once in a while.

Let's say your employee is struggling with a project you handed him. Just ask, 'What do you need right now?'

And he might say, 'I need Helen from accounts to give me the true budget for this project.'

Bingo.

Your daughter is in her first romantic relationship and is upset about her first argument with her girlfriend. You are trying to make her feel better by sharing a story about your first argument, but it is not really working. Instead you ask her, 'What do you need right now?' And she says, 'I need a hug.'

What do you need right now?

If you know the answer, give it to yourself or ask someone who can give it to you.

Kate's asking story

It is asking for the little but important things in relationships that often leave me vulnerable and scared to act.

Many years ago, when I was in my thirties and after my first marriage ended, I went on a date with a guy after not having dated anyone in a long time. We were sitting opposite each other on a bench seat. I remember the place – it was a casual outdoors bar that was usually very busy but not many people had arrived yet.

My date and I were chatting, but he couldn't seem to look at me much at all. He was talking, but looking around a lot. I knew this guy – we were already friends – and even though it was probably because he was feeling nervous, his behaviour was strange and was making me feel uncomfortable.

I thought, 'This is ridiculous. Is it me or him? Am I misinterpreting this?'

As usual, my low self-esteem with men started me second-guessing my feelings, but then something clicked and I realised that whether it was him or me, I wasn't going to sit there for hours with someone who wouldn't even look at me.

Looking back, what happened next was a big moment for me.

I got up the courage and said, 'Are you okay, James?'

'Yes,' he said.

'Oh, good,' I said. 'Because you keep looking around a lot – everywhere but at me. Can you please look at me when I talk to you?'

I did it! I asked for respectful behaviour from a man and I survived!

Everything changed for me from then on.

When I thought about why I felt so vulnerable in this kind of situation, I worked out it was because an early boyfriend I had when I was 19, whom I absolutely adored, broke up with me because he said I was hard work and too demanding.

I probably was pretty hard work back then – weren't we all at that age? But from then on, I decided that the key to making relationships work was to be less demanding and not ask for much.

Considering how long ago that was and how many years of practice I'd had at not asking for respect, the moment in this story – even though it was over in 30 seconds – was monumental for me.

By backing myself and asking for basic respect, I had drawn a line in the sand. My actions had sent a message out to the world: I am worthy of happiness in relationships! Taking action raised my self-esteem, and that gave me more courage to ask, as well as the confidence to follow my instincts in the moment.

Fast forward many years and I am now happily married with two children. Being a mum has been a gift in learning to ask. After I suffered mild postnatal depression after my second girl was born, I realised it would be damaging for us all, and especially the children, if I didn't ask for help.

I got to work asking everyone over to help with dinner, or asking if we could please visit because I needed help. When people offered help, I said yes.

My depression came as a result of having two children only 14 months apart, but as long as I had things planned and people around, I was fine.

I am lucky, actually, because isolation among mothers is a terrible problem. So I am very grateful that it became an understanding in our family that my needs as a woman were vital for the good of all.

To this day, when I ask for a day off to do something for myself, my husband supports my needs and there is no guilt. Too many mothers accept their lot and lose sight of their personal happiness and become martyrs.

Learning to ask for time and money to do what you desire is not indulgent or selfish, it is vital to the welfare and atmosphere of the family home. I highly recommend it.

Kate, 50

Chapter 25

Asking to become better

Personally, I think some of the best asks are the ones that allow us to become better versions of ourselves.

Better lovers, better partners, better friends, better employers, better employees, better students, better neighbours, better parents.

I believe we are capable of getting better at most things, but we need to ask where we can improve and what we might be doing wrong.

Of course, the answers to these questions are not always easy to hear or accept, which is why we often shy away from asking them.

You may think you are a good neighbour, but how do you know? You may think you are doing a great job at work, but how do you know? You may believe your marriage is going well, but how do you know?

Regular check-ins

A practice my husband and I have been doing regularly is to check in with each other on how we are tracking as spouses.

For a long time when I asked him how I was going as his wife, he would say, 'I am happy. Nothing to report.' And I would feel proud, and maybe even a little smug.

Until the day he said, 'Actually, I would like you to support me a bit more.'

Not so proud or smug.

I could feel my heart sink a little, but then I remembered I had asked him the question so that I could be the wife I wanted to be.

If I had gotten defensive when he told me he needed more support from me, I would have said, 'Well, you did not support me when…', which never ends well.

I then asked him how I could support him more, and asked him to describe what that would look like for him. And he told me.

The incredible thing is that what he needed in terms of support from me was not even on my radar. What support looks like to him and what it looks like to me are completely different. There was no way I would have known what he needed to feel supported if I had not asked him.

I started supporting him the way he asked me to, and the next time we spoke about it he mentioned the difference it had made for him through a very busy time at work.

Now we nail it down regularly by asking each other: 'How can I support you best this week?'

We have learned to not assume that what is needed one week is needed the following week – sometimes I need more support, sometimes he needs more; it changes.

This asking has made a huge difference to our marriage. It allows us to fully understand what each of us needs to feel supported in different areas of our lives, both as a couple and as individuals and parents.

Less guessing, more asking

Many of us spend a lot of time guessing what is needed from us in our relationships and at work. But while we spend a lot of energy trying our hardest, our energy and care is wasted if it is not what is required of us.

You may think that what your teenage son needs you to do is his washing, but he would actually feel supported if you helped him with his homework.

You may think that your latest employee needs flexible work arrangements, but what she actually may want is more responsibility and autonomy.

You may think that your best friend wants a splashy birthday party with lots of people, but actually they just want to watch their favourite movie at home with their closest friends.

Where are you guessing and where are you asking?

Unless we ask what others need, we cannot know what is needed.

And, of course, it goes the other way around – unless we say what we need, how can the people around us know what to give us?

Where in your life are you guessing and hoping for the best, and where in your life are you asking?

Asking is the key to a more fulfilling life.

Chapter 26
Asking for support

There are many helping professionals out there who are just waiting to be asked. But it can be hard to know exactly what support or help we may need at a particular time.

Below is a very simple overview (an edited version of the information available on the International Coaching Federation website, coachfederation.org/) to give you a better understanding of some of the professional options that exist to support you.

Different approaches

Coaching

Supporting personal and professional growth based on change you initiate yourself in pursuit of specific outcomes, coaching is future focused. While challenging feelings/emotions may be a natural outcome of coaching, the primary focus is on creating actionable strategies for achieving specific goals in one's work or personal life.

The emphases in a coaching relationship are on action, accountability and follow through.

Therapy

Dealing with pain, dysfunction and conflict within an individual or in relationships, therapy is about healing. The focus is often on resolving difficulties arising from the past that hamper an individual's emotional functioning in the present, improving overall psychological functioning, and dealing with the present in more emotionally healthy ways.

Consulting

Individuals or organisations 'retain' consultants for their expertise – they call them in when needed. While consulting approaches vary widely, the assumption is the consultant will diagnose problems and prescribe and, sometimes, implement solutions.

Mentoring

A mentor is an expert who provides wisdom and guidance based on his or her own experience. Mentoring may include advising, counselling and coaching.

Go ahead and ask

It is possible to work with all the professionals introduced above at the same time because, as you can see, they all offer different services. But if you know you need more support to live the life you want to live, the best way to find out what is right for you is to ask. Yes, that again!

Chapter 27
Paying it forward

So there are many, many gifts in asking for what we need and want. I hope that by this point in my book you have experienced this for yourself in both small and larger ways.

It does take courage to ask, there is no doubt about that, but it also takes courage to share the gift of asking with others, too.

One way we can pay forward the gift of asking is to respond to someone's complaints about life.

So when you find yourself in a situation with a family member, friend or colleague where they are complaining to you about something in their life, with compassion and grace you can ask, 'Have you asked for what you need?'

Sometimes the answer will be, 'Yes, I have,' and that may give way to more complaining.

So, with compassion and grace, you can then ask, 'What do you need right now?'

Of course, this will not allow you to fix anything for them. As hard as we might try, and many of us try very hard, we are unable to fix anything for anyone – not in a way that is sustainable or empowering for them. But what you may be able to do in asking these questions is create a space for them to gain clarity or insight about their current situation. Not as a coach, but as a friend – as someone who wants to see them in a better place.

The shifting itself needs to be done by them, though, as we are all capable of solving our own issues; sometimes we just need support to do so.

Share your story

Another way to pay forward the gift of asking is to share your personal stories of asking for what you need and want with other women in your life.

And not just the success stories.

It is sometimes the stories with a twist that have the most impact: 'I did not get what I asked for, but I learned that I did not want to be part of that group anyway, and I would not have known that unless I had asked the question in the first place.'

Sharing your stories of asking and showing other people how to ask are reminders to you to keep asking as well – a kind of booster shot. So as you share the important gift of asking with others, you reinforce the habit of asking in yourself, too.

Chapter 28
The universe says

One of my favourite quotes about asking involves believing in a higher power of some sort. It goes like this:

The universe has only three answers:

1. *Yes*
2. *Not yet*
3. *I have something better in mind*

If you chose to believe that everything you could ask for only had these three answers, what could you ask for?

Chapter 29
The last ask

So here we are at the final pages of this book.

What is your relationship to asking now? What has had the biggest impact on you? Do you have a different asking story to when you first started?

Reading *The Gift of Asking* will have given you insights into the many levels of asking, but as I said at the beginning, you will gain the most by taking action and asking.

Insight can change us internally; action changes us internally and externally.

I hope that you will honour the time you have taken to read this book by holding your asking list in hand and stepping boldly out into the world.

As you come to the last pages of this book, I have an ask of you.

As women we are incredibly powerful – we can nourish and nurture, we can build and create, we can connect and heal.

My ask of you is to be all of these things for yourself:

>*Nourish yourself.*
>
>*Nurture yourself.*
>
>*Build and create for yourself.*
>
>*Connect with and heal yourself.*
>
>*You are worthy of everything you need and want.*
>
>*Allow yourself.*

And in that allowing, allow your mothers, daughters, sisters, friends, aunties and all women around you to allow themselves, too.

Because when we practise being worthy through the action of asking, we become worthy. And when women become worthy together, we are unstoppable.

My final ask of you is, ASK.

Postscript
Let's stay connected

I thank you for reading *The Gift of Asking*, and my wish is that it has elevated you in your own eyes.

Remember to download your free resources to support you to navigate and explore your asking journey. Go to kemibooks.com to get yours.

If this book has made a difference to your life in some way, I would love to hear from you.

If you would like to know about my work or how to work with me, please go to kemi.courses, and while you're there download 'Your Self-Coaching Checklist'.

You can also connect with me via:

- LinkedIn: keminekvapil
- Instagram: @keminekvapil
- Podcast: *The Shift Series*

Thank you.

With thanks

To my husband, Emrys, for his conscious support in so many ways and for choosing to partner with me. It is a gift that we can support each other's dreams.

To Lisette, I could not have written this book, or work the way that I do, without you doing your work with such skill and grace. I am so blessed to have you on my team. Your support and partnership will never be taken for granted.

To all of the women in this book who have generously shared aspects of their lives as a contribution to others. Your beauty and words have raised this book higher.

To my clients who have courageously taken on asking for what they need and demonstrated the powerful effect of asking. You inspire me daily and it is a privilege to work with you.

To my coach, Belinda MacInnes, for the space you create for me to 'be' with no judgement.

To my writing partner, Samantha Gash, thank you for the beach house, the runs, the silence, the brainstorming, the dancing and the laughter.

To Lucy Tumanow-West, my editor, for saying yes to my ask of being my editor again, and for saying yes to a crazy deadline. You truly are a blessing.

To you, the reader, with so many things competing for your attention, I thank you for choosing to read this book as a good way to use your time.

Extract from _POWER_
by Kemi Nekvapil

About Power

'_The most common way people give up their
power is by thinking they don't have any._'
– Alice Walker

Women today have more opportunities than our mothers and grandmothers ever had, and yet the societal structures we must navigate to claim and own some of these opportunities can still lead us to question our abilities and our power. For many women, 'power' is abstract. Many of us have been and continue to be intimidated by it. Throughout this book you will find that I have not used concepts of 'soft power' or 'personal power'. This is deliberate. Power is power. We do not need to 'feminise it' to make it more palatable; we need to redefine it. I want us to reacquaint ourselves with this word in a positive way.

Countless women were raised like me to believe that power belongs to others, that it is destructive and therefore they had no interest in exploring or owning power for themselves. My relationship to power has mainly been one of _powerlessness_.

In my experience, power was white – either a white man in a suit, or a white woman who was blonde and thin. A university education also meant power – if you had a degree, you had more power than someone who didn't. Being able to get a university education was linked to privilege, which was linked to whiteness, which in turn was linked to power.

At school I was black, female and overweight, and a university degree was not an option for me. Power, as it appeared to me then, was not a concept I recognised for myself. Over time I have needed to explore and define power on my own terms.

Julie Diamond is a woman whose work I admire when it comes to the subject of power – she is a leadership coach who has spent more than thirty years working in the world of human and organisational change. She is also the author of *Power: A User's Guide*, in which she writes: 'Power is neither good nor bad; it is energy, a human drive to shape the world, influence others, and make an impact. We need power. Power may be difficult to master, but it's vital to have. It's generative and creative.'

I like her explanation of power; it's so much more inclusive than what I had experienced or been led to believe. Add to that the *Oxford English Dictionary* definition of power – 'the ability or capacity to do something or act in a particular way' – and we have something positive to work with. We all have the ability to do something or act in a particular way. So power is for all of us; it is not for the select few.

In my book *The Gift of Asking*, I talk about the struggle many women have with asking for what they need and want. One of the reasons for this struggle is the belief that to ask is to rock the boat, to no longer be seen as a 'good girl'. Being 'good' – not asking for more, pleasing others, doing what we are told, and looking 'good' – is a way for women to hold ourselves and each other powerless.

I have coached hundreds of women in my one-to-one practice and thousands of women in group settings. These are women in

CEO roles, women running their own companies, entrepreneurs, managers, women on the land, professional athletes, yoga teachers, activists, social workers and coaches – women in various positions in diverse industries. Rarely do these women start working with me to explore their power, but in the coaching process most uncover their relationship with power in the same way they uncover their relationship to asking. They explore the times they owned their power, when they had their power taken away, when they gave it away, how they have stepped into their power and how life changes when they own and harness that power.

I am writing this book now at a place in my life where I am no longer going to pretend I don't have any power. And I am definitely no longer interested in being a good girl. And my intention is that by the end of this book, you'll step out of your version of being a 'good girl' and step into becoming a fully expressed woman.

Power that is created by a system based on a person's gender, privilege and 'granted' status makes us believe it only belongs to a chosen few. And the continuity of this system depends on the chosen few inviting others who look like them and have the same upbringing as them to the power table. The rest of us are excluded. If you are reading this book, you are undoubtedly one of 'the rest of us' and you know how the system works. You know how it affects us every day – the world we live in has been set up to keep us small. For many years I heard 'The system is broken', but this is a rose-coloured way of looking at things. It gives the impression that there was once, in the 'days of old', a system that served everyone equally, and somehow one day, or even over a period of time, that system collapsed. But let's take off the rose-coloured glasses, and confront the truth. The system was meant to be this way; nothing got broken. The system was set up for men, it was set up for whiteness. And the tragedy is that within that system, many of us have felt broken.

Whether you are reading this as a woman, a woman of colour, a queer woman, a non-binary person, or a disabled woman, you know. We all know what it feels like to be told we are broken. We internalise these myths – and when we do, we are complicit in the system and we keep ourselves exactly where we are told we belong.

I have learnt, as many women have, how to live and lead 'as an apology'. Let me clarify what I mean here:

- I learnt how to make myself small by not sharing my opinions, for fear of not being liked, because we are led to believe that being liked is our most important value.
- I learnt to pretend I didn't have needs and wants because I didn't want to be told I was needy or difficult.
- I learnt how to be a 'good girl', to only do what was expected of me and toe the line.
- I learnt how to apologise when speaking, diminishing the power of my words by smiling, or giggling 'to soften my meaning' or my voice, or by actually apologising before I spoke: 'I'm sorry to say this, but…'
- I learnt how to deny my leadership capabilities because my mind was fraught with the possibility of judgement and failure.
- I learnt how to live 'as an apology' as a black woman navigating predominantly white spaces.

This was my version of living and leading as an apology. What does your version look like?

In contrast, what does living and leading *without* apology look like?

- It means that we take up space, without apology.
- It means that we communicate our needs because we are worthy of having our needs met.
- It means we operate in the world as full expressions of ourselves, creating our own unique paths.
- It means we own our opinions and voices, without diminishment or apology.
- It means that if we want leadership, we can step into leadership knowing that judgement and failure are part of the deal.
- It means that if we are called to leadership, we don't assume we are not good enough. We understand we will learn as we go.
- It means that we stand proud in our racial identity and ethnicity, and support others to do the same.

Now is the time to elevate our individual power and the power of other women, because the world needs women to own their power like never before. It is time we own our ability to 'do something or act in a particular way', to build a better system from the inside out.

The shift from external to internal

I wrote this book to show you how I shifted the Power Stories I had about myself, so you can do the same with your own Power Stories.

Let's start by thinking about 'external' power.

In 2019, I trained with Dr Brené Brown to be a facilitator of her Dare to Lead™ leadership program. Brené Brown is a research professor and her work focuses on shame, vulnerability and courage. She talks about the 'power over' model, where people use shame and fear to wield *power over* others. We can see the results of this form of power everywhere, across the world, and the results of the fear of losing that perceived power. This is a power that sits outside of oneself. It can be taken away at any moment, which is why the wielders of this form of power hold onto it so tightly. Their perception of their own power is so fragile they need to use shame and fear to keep hold of it.

We don't need more of this kind of power in the world and historically this form of power is created and perpetuated by men. Even back in the eighteenth century, the English writer, philosopher and women's rights advocate Mary Wollstonecraft recognised this, declaring, 'I do not wish women to have power over men; but power over themselves.'

This form of power has led us to believe that there is only so much power to go around. In this system, if you have power, I can't have it, and vice versa. Many women who work or have worked within patriarchal structures have seen this form of power play out in every way. Some of these women were smart enough to know that they would need to play the 'power game' to achieve their career ambitions. But to succeed, they had to perpetuate the idea that power was scarce and they 'needed to protect their patch' – and perhaps as a result they were not able or willing to support other women in their careers. On top of that, the women 'in power' would have felt isolated in a structure that was not built for women to thrive. There are many downsides to this type of power.

But power does not have to be an external force. When power is an *internal* force, it is an abundant resource: I can have it and you can have it too.

*

Discover a
new favourite

Visit **penguin.com.au/readmore**